Book of Wonders in Poetry
by GEORGE L. HAND

Wonders are there for all to see.
As everyone should know, most are free.

iUniverse LLC
Bloomington

BOOK OF WONDERS IN POETRY

iUniverse books may be ordered through booksellers or by contacting:

iUniverse LLC
1663 Liberty Drive
Bloomington, IN 47403
www.iuniverse.com
1-800-Authors (1-800-288-4677)

ISBN: 978-1-4917-3253-3 (sc)
ISBN: 978-1-4917-3254-0 (e)

Printed in the United States of America.

iUniverse rev. date: 04/30/2014

Dedication

I dedicate this book with love to all my kin.
You're the greatest family that has ever been.

Introduction

We read Walt Whitman's poems in class.
The word "wonder" described a youth and a lass.
It was reused concerning the arm and other body parts.
He was also impressed with crafts and arts.
Of course, his ideas were appropriate for the age.
How much did anyone know at that stage?
Since the mid 19thn century, knowledge has grown so fast.
We understand so much more now than we did in the past.
Human knowledge flows at an expanding rate.
Yet how much don't we know? It is our fate.
Personally, it's all completely awesome to me.
Every science presents more for us to see.
Whitman was awed by the star filled sky.
Now we know some stars have planets orbiting by.
We know about galaxies, their distance away.
Star composition, a super nova on its dying day.
Life is even more awesome on our earth.
All animal and plant life has wondrous worth.
In my own life I've seen so much
Noticing insects, rodents, birds and such.
I think of man. In the past he has done great things,
Taming nature and reaping the benefit this brings.
Maybe the most wonderful of all is man
With his ability to wonder and think he can.

Contents

Chapter 1. Animal Wonders

The first four chapters describe wonders to me.
Little stories about animals pulled from memory.
Most people don't notice things that are wild.
I'm old but I still see with eyes of a child.

Megafauna are big animals. Think about deer.
May they always be plentiful giving us cheer.

1. Animal Emotions

Some scholars will claim animals have no emotions.
It's wishful thinking to have such silly notions.
It's called anthropomorphism, applying humanity that way.
Only survival and reproduction count they say.
A cat wants to be fed when she purrs on your lap.
I call it love, though maybe I'm a sap.
My dog welcomes me by racing around.
This is happiness. No other explanation can be found.
Each of our dogs has shown emotions, it's so neat.
They have to sneeze and rub their noses between their feet.
We've come home and with one look we can tell.
"Okay, what did you do?" Guilt shows so well.
Sophie mouthed three toys at once. She had to try.
"Look at me," she'd prance with tail held high.
That shows emotion we'd call pride.
No other explanation fits. Do the experts chide?
Stories about animals' grief are classic tales.
When their "Master" dies, their pining never pales.

Raised hackles show anger and fear.
Telling other animals and people, don't come near.
How do you explain cross species attraction?
Especially cats and dogs where you'd expect fighting action.
There are crying elephants when a colleague dies.
They even touch their friend saying their goodbyes.
The best example of animal emotions, I saw on TV,
The reaction of a baby hippo showing glee.
He was so happy, his "handler" was coming to him.
His whole body wagged. Four legs pumped with vim.
This is a sign of love that anybody can see.
Animals do have emotions, we all should agree.

2. Instinct

Complicated behavior by animals is a wonder to me.
We explain it as instinctive. How else should it be?
Bees probably have the best record for their size.
When one finds suitable flowers where it flies,
It remembers their location and how to get there.
It directs other bees to the source with care.
Independent of wind, they can find their way home.
This allows them freedom of where they roam.
They know their jobs and make the hive hum.
With their micro brains you'd expect them to be dumb.
Birds build nests each according to its kind,
Instinctively though the location they must find.
Spiders make their complicated webs in less than a day,
Exquisitely designed to catch their prey.
Behavior is determined by instinct it seems.
Which means, it is written in their genes.
I'd like to hear someone has found the spot

In the genome where the instructions are gotten.
A Nobel Prize for the discovery would be a good shot.

3. Fifty Years of Change

We've been here for over fifty years.
The fauna have rapidly changed including the deer.
We used to see raccoons and skunks at night.
Skunks are much too slow in their flight.
Hence the dead bodies by the side of the road.
The drivers should have braked or at least slowed.
Opossums have moved north and were here a bit.
Also, being slow moving, they often were hit.
Rabies was transmitted and took it's toll.
Mid-size animals died, destruction on a roll.
When we got here, there were no Canada geese.
There was quite a stir with the first sighting of these.
People stopped by the side of the road to look.
Soon geese were filling each cranny and nook.
Some places they became a real pain in the —,
Especially on golf courses, droppings covered the grass.
In later years their numbers dropped a lot.
Most likely because coyotes arrived on the spot.
We never saw a turkey back in the day.
They've also moved in, and are here to stay.
People say they've seen the fisher cat.
It's a giant weasel, something like that.
More hawks are around. Small things watch out.
They're taking care of rodents no doubt.
It looks like evening up is nature's goal.
Except for the deer. Multiplying is their role.
We've had as many as nine behind the house.
They eat shrubs. I like wild things, so I won't grouse.

4. Tracks in the Snow

After the new snow falls, I like to check the tracks.
There's the little bird ones skittering forth and back.
Squirrels are easy, starting and stopping at a tree.
They're searching for the acorns from the fall burying spree.
I've spotted fox though maybe they're fisher cat.
They're not in my old scout book, nothing like that.
Coyotes are easy. They're just like my dog.
Except they travel straight, no sniffing each bush and log.
Deer have their distinguishing two toed track.
They don't travel single file though together in a pack.
In southern New England tracks disappear fast.
Snow melting by day means they don't last.
When the snow melts down, there's something I've found.
Tunnels wandering about on the surface of the ground.
I presume these are from mice, voles, or moles.
Maybe they find seeds or dead insects far from their holes.
They certainly can't burrow with ground frozen hard.
Though I can't see anything edible in my yard.

5. Surprises

Anyone who walks in the woods has had the surprise.
As a kid, I was walking point. I thought I'd die.
A deer jumped up. She'd been sleeping right there.
Both of us were startled being completely unaware.
I've surprised several. One snorted and they ran away.
They can hear quite well. They were sleeping that day.
I was fishing once and saw where the cat tails were apart.
I could get close to the water when I got a start.
A great blue heron was standing at that spot.

4

Sudden flapping could cause heart failure like as not.
In comparison turkeys seem like nothing much at all.
Twice they've flown straight up, pine trees quite tall.
Startled by turkeys? You'd think I'd get warned by my dog.
To her they seemed as interesting as a log.
The best story, I was picking black berries out back.
I parted the bushes to avoid a thorn attack.
I reached in and was about to touch a snake.
Pulling back I moved away fast for goodness sake.
Of all species, snakes give us the biggest shock.
Their sudden movement, your heart sinks, your knees knock.
To many, the chance of a snake, they'll always take stock.
"Do you want to walk in the woods or by the lake out there?"
"Only if you'll guarantee no snakes, I get such a scare."

6. Survival in the Snow

We've had more than normal snow this year.
It's been cold enough so little has melted clear.
Below the surface is a layer of icy snow,
Making it difficult to walk, too hard a go.
I watched three deer sampling shrubs out back.
They walked carefully. Their legs might crack.
Place a hoof, then put on weight to break through.
This seemed a reasonable thing to do.
I hoped they would have no need to run.
A broken limb and that deer would be done.
I got to thinking about survival in our wood.
I know animals manage. Their odds aren't good.
Birds that are ground feeders must change diets.

Breaking through that snow, too hard to try it.
Maybe the doves, nuthatches and chickadees
Find insect eggs and bushes bearing seeds.
The poor turkeys, on the other hand, must make do.
Scratching for food, can they break through?
Most rodents save food in their lairs,
While squirrels bury nuts. Do they know where?
If they dig down chances are, it won't be there.
With winter so tough it's a wonder any survive.
Their hope for survival, spring will soon arrive.

7. Going to Die

We've all read about wild animals when death is near.
They're sick or wounded. The ending seems clear.
They'll look for a secluded place out of sight,
And wait for their passage into the long night.
Maybe it's built in, to have a peaceful death,
Avoid the pain of predators at your last breath.
Domestic animals seem to have this trait still.
Our dog Smokey showed signs of feeling ill.
At that time our pets were free to roam,
And one day our old dog didn't come home.
Thinking of nature, did she crawl off to die?
Maybe the woods at the corner was where she'd lie.
I started looking. Sure enough, there was our pet.
"Come on old girl. Lets go home. It's not time yet."
We walked home slowly. By hand she was fed.
We chose living while nature said dead.
As she aged, bad hips meant she couldn't arise.
She put her weight on her front legs to our surprise.
When she could no longer climb stairs to the door,
I built a ramp for her. I would have done more.

Then life was just too hard, We knew the score.

8. Frolicking Whales

We thought a whale watch would make a nice day trip.
It's only an hour to Gloucester where there are several ships.
Captain Bob claimed we'd get out there fast.
Stellwagen bank is where whales have their repast.
They guarantee money back if no whale is sighted.
We had read they're around. This day should be right.
There were several ships. All were staying clear.
You don't pester the whales by approaching too near.
A mom and her calf swam near our boat.
The curious calf had never seen anything afloat.
I know from an environmental view this is not okay.
Still it's fascinating to us land lubbers in every way.
Captain Bob slowly steered away from the family group.
Then took off at a high speed. All wondering what's the scoop.
Other boats gathered around. What was the fuss?
Two whales were putting on a show for us.
They'd dive below then sail into the air,
Causing a tremendous splash, spray everywhere.
They rolled and with flukes and fins slapped.
We were all so fascinated, some even clapped.
A marine biologist aboard talked about the whales.
She had to admit, this was beyond the pale.
These were two males competing or at play,
A courtship ritual or they're showing off this way.
We felt so lucky witnessing this unknown event,
With the expert not aware of what it all meant.
Sometimes nature surprises us with a wonder sent.

9. The Hard Place

"Mama says, 'Be careful of the hard place.'
Why is it there? No trees grow on that space.
Mama says, 'When there's noise, stay back.
Stay back with bright light. It's better black.'
Mama teaches me always be careful, ABC.
Now it is quiet and dark as it should be.
I'll cross the hard place now it's night.
Oh, I hear noise. I see bright light.
I must go back. No, I must run."
Bam! "Mama, I hurt everywhere. I'm all done."
"Damn deer. Smashed my bumper and grill.
He seemed frozen there he was so still.
Why didn't he move? I have to wonder why."
Why didn't you slow down? He didn't have to die.

10. Dolphins

We have observed dolphins at Sea World type places.
They are smart, quite trainable and have sweet faces.
The curve of their mouths is a perpetual smile.
If you're inclined, you can swim with them for a while.
Other aquariums are around, comparable or less so.
Few people see them in the wide ocean though.
We were lucky on two occasions as I'll explain.
One was a whale watch off Bar Harbor, Maine.
It was rather a bust concerning whales,
Only a few distant blows, no fins or tails.
The dolphins filled in, welcoming us to sea.
There must have been 500 cavorting playfully.
They were clearly playing. None searching for a meal.
Certainly the trip was worthwhile. We got a good deal.

We traveled the inside passage off Alaska's coast.
Whenever we go places, I like to see the most.
Part of the trip was out of the sight of land.
So I watched the bow wave and saw something grand.
A dolphin was riding the wave like surfers do.
Except they could ride as long as they chose to.
Intelligent animals like to play. It's so nice.
I observed this wonderful activity twice.

11. Pronghorn

The academic article made an interesting claim.
That ancient man had the stamina to run down game.
Maybe an antelope would collapse in African heat,
While man has a cooling system that can't be beat.
However, man is essentially the same today,
And no one in Africa hunts this way.
The young man read the article. He'd put it to the test.
He and his wife were traveling out west.
He saw a pronghorn by the road's side.
"I'm going to test the theory," he said with pride.
"Don't be silly," his wife responded too late.
Her husband ran off at a fast gait.
After an hour he stumbled back to the car.
He was hot and exhausted. He'd run too far.
Now about the pronghorn which is really a goat.
There are two facts which he didn't take note.
Speed second to the cheetah, stamina of a horse,
No human could compare to this wonder of course.

12. Elephant Seals

We were on our California vacation, my wife and I.
The Big Sur is a highway everyone should try.
This is a remote section of coast, a spectacular drive
Between mountains and the sea, it makes you feel alive.
We were satisfied just taking in the view.
Others considered it a trial to go through.
Especially the motor cycle crowd who caused us concern
By laying out almost flat taking the hairpin turns.
We finished our drive none the less for wear.
The road was straight and level leaving there.
We came upon dozens of cars parked by the sea.
This wasn't a swimmers beach. What could it be?
We stopped to investigate though not planned.
Hundreds of elephant seals were asleep on the sand.
Looking like giant fish, dead and washed ashore,
They were waiting to molt and nothing more.
In various groupings, the seals come here.
Adolescent males had this time of year.
We watched as two decided to have a fight.
They reared up and crashed chests to show their might.
After two wacks, enough, to hell with it.
Sleep is better than conflict, so they quit.
What a pleasant interlude, a complete surprise.
Willing to check out the unforseen is wise.

13. The Raccoon

I heard barking down in the woody corner lot.
It sounded like our dog Smokey like as not.
She wasn't a barker normally. Something was amiss.
I decided I better walk on down and investigate this.

It was Smokey barking at a raccoon on the ground.
Which was completely unconcerned I found.
The raccoon showed its contempt for my dog and me
By walking away and doing a trick for us to see.
It did a forward roll showing us its back side.
It knew it was safe, no need to run and hide.
I looked at poor Smokey with scratches about her eyes.
The raccoon was being kind. No reason for anyone to die.
I've read a raccoon can gut a dog full grown.
This one could have blinded ours all on its own.
I certainly was glad I investigated that day.
The plus was the raccoon acting in a strange way.
For some reason it was unafraid and wanted to play.

14. Smokey and the Skunk

I heard continuous barking from across the way.
What had gotten into Smokey. I hoped she was okay.
Looking out I saw by the street light's glow,
Our dog confronting a skunk. Oh, no!
The skunk gave a warning by stomping its feet.
Smokey just wanted it to leave our street.
I called but alas it was to no avail.
The skunk thought, enough, and raised its tail.
Skunk dousing is an experience all should miss.
If I didn't relate its foulness, I'd be remiss.
No way would we let Smokey into the house.
She slept on the porch. I felt like a louse.
The next day we made a call to our vet.
Suggestion: a tomato juice bath would be a good bet.
We tried the remedy. It worked quite well.
Of course, the porch also smelled like hell.
I hosed off both dog and porch that day,

Though the skunk odor wouldn't go away.
We could smell traces of the odor six months more.
Ah, skunk stink each time we went through the door.
How do you explain a characteristic like this?
Evolutionists claim it's all chance, easy to dismiss.
I consider it another wonder, my naive bliss.

15. Watch for Moose*

"Watch for moose," the road signs say.
Because making contact will ruin your day.
The state isn't worried much about the moose,
But the havoc that one could let loose.
A car will drive under one, it's so tall.
Of car occupants, it could kill them all.
The young man was sensible. He was aware,
As he drove down the dirt road with care.
Suddenly, from the bushes a moose came forth.
The driver was able to stop of course.
The moose felt challenged. He was of the male gender.
So he came up to the car and sat on the fender.
Then his honor satisfied, he calmly walked away.
Fortunately, not much damage requiring cash outlay.
The youth had a great answer to, "How was your day?"
* My son's true experience

16. Howling

Coyotes arrived in our town a few years ago.
They have adapted and know how to stay low.
I suppose it's natural for them to fear man.
They have no other enemies in this crowded land.
Unfortunately, they have found one source of food.

Outdoor cats are rare in each neighborhood.
We used to see signs describing a kitty lost.
It's so sad for each family, but it's nature's cost.
I've only seen coyotes a few times, once in our yard,
Though many tracks in the snow say keep guard.
They're not likely to attack me unless rabidly mad.
Though they could go after my dog, an easy meal to be had.
Once I heard them in the evening in woods nearby.
A mom and her grown pups hunting. I heard the cry.
It was a mixture of wolf and hyena laugh.
Enough to give you an eerie feeling and a half.
The next night an ambulance with a siren went by.
It was odd, but the coyotes answered the cry.
Maybe this was their God, the great coyote in the sky.

17. The Deer

Deer seem to be a constant in our suburban town.
There's no hunting. Nothing keeps their numbers down.
Twice last winter we had nine in the yard.
My wife wouldn't let me scare them. It's not too hard.
They took a bite of a shrub here, then there.
Not too much lost. They seem to eat with care.
They all seemed healthy. Not one was skin and bones.
Which makes me wonder. What do they eat on their own?
In my walks out back in several acres of wood,
I've never seen evidence of their using anything for food.
No browsing on annual plants, shrubs, or tree bark.
Nothing seems to be bitten or has teeth marks.
'Tis one mystery. I'll add another one for thought.
Except for one antlered buck, I've seen naught.

Do the males hide during the rutting season?
This seems odd. Could rare hunters be the reason?
Behind my son's home is where I saw the one.
He walked slowly. We couldn't see him if he didn't run.
After passing he picked up to a regular pace.
Somehow he reasoned, we wouldn't give chase.

18. The Baby Chimp

By watching his mom the baby chimp learned,
What he should pick and eat, what should be spurned.
He also learned what could be used as a tool.
A rock the right size was pretty cool.
This was the chimp invention for cracking nuts.
It was almost foolproof if you weren't a putz.
Place the nut on a hard surface so it wouldn't roll.
Hitting the nut with the rock just right was the goal.
The baby held the rock just right with both hands.
Not smashing your fingers was a good plan.
He swung the rock and each time he'd miss.
He stopped and looked at the rock, "What's this?
The rock must be defective. I'll throw it away.
I did it just like mom. This isn't my day."
So the young chimp tried a different rock.
No thought of his aim, he gave another sock.

19. Behind Bars

I hate to see intelligent animals under lock and key.
They're used to foraging with family and living free.
Zoos are the worst since there's nothing to do.
Even the most enlightened managers haven't a clue.
The adult male gorilla, usually a cause of dread,

Sat, his security blanket draped over shoulders and head.
The keeper came with the big guy's daily treat,
A jar of pureed baby food, necessary meat.
From a spoon between the bars the gorilla ate.
When it was gone, he flipped his blanket in an agitated state.
With pellets the keeper filled his food bowl.
While he sat under his blanket, a gloomy soul.
Then a wonder, a tiny mouse approached the food.
As he took a piece, it lightened the sad sack's mood.
The gorilla watched as the mouse scampered away.
He tossed a pellet, a token of thanks for making his day.

Cute little babies come to mind when we think of chimps.
They cling to their moms, or play, or act like imps.
However, adult males are fierce and can cause harm.
It's said one could pull off a big man's arm.
A large number of people had come to the zoo.
The primate house attracted more than a few.
The big chimp put on a show. He beat his chest.
He did a somersault and bellowed at the guests.
Quite a crowd was attracted around his cage,
Then they got a small taste of the prisoner's rage.
He took a great mouthful of water and sprayed the crowd.
Then bellowed at them in a voice quite loud.
I presume the big chimp acted this way
Because he was mad as hell. He'd make man pay.
Or else he'd gone insane on an earlier day.

Chapter 2. Small Mammals

The small mammals seem to always be around.
Watch them. Their ingenuity will truly astound.

1. Kamikaze Squirrel

We got a new bird feeder. It should be the right kind.
It's mounted on a metal pole. The squirrels won't dine.
Every day I learn new stuff. Here's something neat.
Besides claws, squirrels have friction pads on their feet.
I replace the metal pole with painted PVC.
This fatter pole should work. I'll have to see.
Drat, I'll smear axle grease. They'll slide.
This seems to help them. It had to be tried.
A sheet metal piece slowed them for a day.
Now they jump from a window screen. They find a way.
So I move the bird feeder farther out.
A nearby rhododendron bush provides a means to flout.
I'm saved temporarily when one chews off the limb.
They're pretty smart rodents though sometimes dim.
Then it's from a limb on an overgrown yew.
I watch and cut off the launch pad, wouldn't you.
Later a squirrel jumped, missed, and crashed.
I watch and he does the same, hopes not dashed.
The fourth try is golden. On the feeder he lands.
I give up. His determined style is just too grand.
It's now a mixed use feeder though not so planned.

2. The Jumping Mouse

We are frugal type people. We save where we can.
When reasonable we buy in bulk as part of the plan.
At the home center bird seed comes in big sacks.
I fortify it with sun flower seed which it tends to lack.
To safeguard it, I mix and store the seed.
A big plastic trash can nicely fills the need.
On lifting the lid one day, I got a minor fright.
A mouse scurried about trying to take flight.
Near the handle I noticed a hole clear through.
I still wonder how it managed to chew.
I carried the full trash can to the front.
Carefully tipping it, I got rid of the runt.
The mouse jumped out and hopped to the woods.
All mice I ever saw scurried as fast as they could.
I looked it up and there are jumping mice.
I wasn't hallucinating which is pretty nice.
I thought a miniature kangaroo rat traveled back east
And stopped in our basement to have a feast.

3. Traveling Mouse

We drove to work by car pool. It's the only way.
It was my friend Grady's turn to drive that day.
We entered the garage at work many stories high.
Park on the same floor, to remember, no need to try.
We pulled into a spot and looked with wonder.
A mouse apparently had made a big blunder.
He crossed the hood by the wiper blades.
I think he was considering the mistake he'd made.
We opened the doors, and he dropped from view.
We ignored him. What else should we do?

Was he the country mouse traveling to the city,
Or just seeking a warm home? For this we felt pity.
If he chose to stay, I hope he found the exit out.
If not, maybe he got back in the country or there about.
I've found evidence of rodents under my car's hood.
They've stored seeds and acorns. You'd expect they would.
None took up residence, though the location seemed good.

4. Mice in the Forrest

The wood out back has a thick layer of debris.
Pine needles and cones or leaves fall from each tree.
Of life this litter doesn't seem to support much.
Though there are chipmunks, squirrels and such.
One day while resting from splitting wood,
I heard the leaves rustling near where I stood.
A mouse stuck out his head. The coast was clear.
It didn't seem to notice the giant so near.
It went about its business. I returned to mine,
Though I filed this encounter for a later time.
I regularly walk our dog, Molly, back there.
Her senses are unbelievable, of all she's aware.
She poked around a hollow in an old tree's base.
I didn't know what she was doing in that place.
Then she wanted to go home. I wasn't sure why.
Since that was her desire, then I would comply.
Protruding from her mouth, I noticed a tail.
I pried open her jaws but to no avail.
The mouse she caught was quite dead.
Our Molly was doing as her instincts said,
The next time I was aware. I pried her jaws that day.
The potential victim dropped and scampered away.

Yet again she poked around but didn't see.
A mouse shot out of the litter and climbed a tree.
I've always been interested in nature. I'm learning still.
All this wonderful life fascinates me. It always will.

5. Bat's Sonar

Bats are a wonder if you think a bit.
For their life as insectivores they really fit.
They're out all night when insects fly high,
And have this ultra sonic call to sweep the sky.
An echo from a tiny mosquito is enough to guide
The bat to its location mouth open wide.
Bats fly with a jerky motion. They never soar.
From dusk to dawn they rest no more.
Once I tried an experiment. I tossed a small rock.
A bat detected it, changed direction, took stock.
In an instant it knew this was no moth.
I had tested the bat's sonar for what it's worth.
Our local bats hibernate for half the year, about.
It's a wonder their survival isn't always in doubt.
Consider the bats we have are tiny as a mouse,
Why do people go nuts if they find one in the house?
They're certainly no danger to you, not a bit.
Just open the windows and doors. Don't have a fit.

6. Chipmunks

Of all the little rodents that live close to us,
I like the chipmunks best, each cute little cuss.
So cheerful, they'll announce their presence with cheeps.
I suppose this tells others, "Away you should keep."

That, or maybe it's to tell the gals,
"Come on over to my burrow, so we can be pals."
Some folks hate them, eating flower bulbs is the rub.
Also, digging their burrows could kill the shrubs.
I never took issue when they ate a tomato or two.
Cherry types are the right size. We had more than a few.
I surprised one in the garden. He had to get away.
When he ran up the inside of a down spout, it made my day.
From up in the gutter he scolded me down below.
I had interrupted his repast. He let me know.
This year I didn't hear the repeated cheeps.
I'd spotted a feral cat. My imagination took a leap.
Damn wild cat took out my furry friends.
I hated the idea of their painful end.
Then a couple of times, I saw a flash of brown.
The chipmunks are smart enough to quiet down.
Maybe they'll get cheerful again when the cat leaves town.

7. Flying Squirrel

I heard the sound. Something crashed down stairs.
It was time to get up anyway, nothing to scare.
I saw a photo tipped over and looked around.
This seemed strange, but that's what made the sound.
Nothing else was amiss. I got my breakfast and sat.
Then I saw a movement. Was that a rat?
It didn't actually jump. More accurately it sailed.
It was a flying squirrel if my eyesight hadn't failed.
Not much bigger than a chipmunk with great big eyes.
I'd only seen one once. That also was a surprise.
Flying squirrels are nocturnal, so they're rarely seen.
This one apparently came down our chimney still clean.

I went to the door and propped it open wide.
Then got the broom to guide it outside.
My maneuver was successful. It went on its way.
My wife would have enjoyed it, but it didn't want to stay.

8. Squirrel Guest

We learn from our mistakes is so true.
A tomato was on the window sill in plain view.
It was there to ripen with window open wide.
Only a screen separated it from outside.
We were out when the squirrel saw an easy meal.
He chewed through the screen with a squirrel's zeal.
On seeing the hole, I knew the culprit with no doubt.
What I didn't know was, did he go out?
I saw some droppings he left on the floor.
Certainly a sign, so I opened the door.
Then I searched the house from room to room,
Bringing my persuader, the trusty kitchen broom.
As I made my rounds, I couldn't spot my prey.
Was he hiding under furniture out of the way?
Then I spotted him on the back of a rocking chair.
His head was stuck between two slats there.
Wondering how I could extract him without a bite.
I realized he didn't move. He was dead from fright.
Is avoiding a painful death so strong in the wild,
That the easier way is taken by the most mild?

9. Fix the Screen

It was summer. The door to the porch was open wide.
This allowed our dog Molly to see the great outside.
She'd bark at the critters that she wanted to scare,

And battered the screen that kept her in there.
I noticed a space with screening pushed away.
I planned to get to it one of these days.
A granddaughter took care of the dog. We had been gone.
On returning we found what had gone wrong.
It seems a squirrel had gotten in through the screen,
And Molly had gone nuts when the varmint was seen.
Doors were opened while Molly was kept at bay.
Hopefully, the squirrel would get out that way.
Presumably, it was gone. Then we got the story.
It had hidden in a couch for which we were sorry.
Our Molly to protect her home and her kin,
Had done all she could to get that thing.
She had torn out the couch end. This couldn't be seen.
Knowing her motivation, to her I wouldn't be mean.
I got heavy duty mesh to cover the porch screen.

10. Ground Squirrels

We went to Las Vegas, a family get together.
It was early January, for Vegas good weather.
Our niece had decided that there she'd marry.
We went to the wedding, and also had time to tarry.
We visited Red Rock Canyon with a few hours to spare.
This is not usually a tourist destination out there.
When visiting a new place, we like to check out the local
scene.
This was a pleasant place to hike, quite serene.
We got out of the car at the parking lot edge.
Only sparse vegetation was among the rocky ledge.
Then the ground seemed to move. With a closer look
Small rodents were coming from every cranny and nook.
They were like pigeons that are fed in the city.

Seeing all the expectant faces I felt pity.
I apologized since we didn't have a scrap of food.
Then another car pulled in, which changed their mood.
Expecting a soft touch, they scampered away.
Strange how wild animals learn to live that way.
Well, adaptability has been known to save the day.

11. Chippy

"There's our little friend. Chippy is his name.
He comes to visit daily. For us it's a game."
We were visiting relatives at their camp ground.
Their frequent visitor was a chipmunk they'd found.
Peanuts in the shell were kept in supply,
Knowing that Chippy would be stopping by.
It's a wonder when a wild thing comes so near.
How do they know they're safe and conquer their fear.
Chippy came right up and took a peanut from her hand.
He carefully covered it with saliva as nature planned.
Apparently, this kept his supply from rotting away.
It would be chipmunk food on a cold winter day.
Chippy tucked a peanut in each cheek pouch,
And a third between his teeth. Chippy was no slouch.
We witnessed several trips. He knew his stuff.
He must've filled his burrow. I'm sure he had enough.
Years later we removed boards from the ground.
It was interesting the remains we found.
We spotted rotted peanuts here and there.
What was left of what Chippy stored with care.
With eyes bigger than his belly he had nuts to spare.

Chapter 3. Bird Wonders

I'm not a birder. They're so serious they make lists.
I watch, so unusual behavior won't be missed.

1. Crossing the Road

Mama duck led her babies across the road.
This was the quickest way to their new abode.
They came from the brook aiming toward the pond.
A better locale of which they'd be more fond.
This was a busy street, much less so late in the day.
I stopped to give the family the right of way.
One duckling stopped not paying attention enough.
Then panicked and caught up, a little ball of fluff.
From behind a car approached probably wondering why,
"Some dummy has stopped. I'll have to pass him by."
I waved out the window, "You idiot, stop."
He realized his impatience was over the top.
Fortunately, for the ducks he braked in time.
If it had ended differently would it be a crime?
I suppose most people would sleep okay
With the knowledge they'd ended a family's days.
The lesson, keep aware of what's in your way.

2. The Swimming Bird

We seek lesser known places, no crowds the plus.
Oak Creek Canyon in Arizona was the attraction for us.
A switchback road took us to the canyon floor.
Water had sculpted it from eons before.
We walked into the state park. A small river flowed.

The current was fast. Nowhere had it slowed.
To take in the spectacular scenery, we sat.
Sometimes the fauna will appear just like that.
Small birds looking for insects hopped along the bank.
Suddenly, one flew a few feet and into the water it sank.
My sweet wife yelled, "Do something quick!"
I should save a bird? I'm not mentally sick.
A few seconds later, it surfaced and flew to the shore.
Apparently, having gotten what it went in for.
The Mrs. was relieved maybe in two ways.
The bird was okay, and it wasn't her hubby's last day.
What a wondrous adaptation and in an arid state too.
This bird could fly underwater like penguins do.
It's called the American dipper though I'm not sure.
My bird book has no mention. Maybe it's too obscure.

3. Canadian Robins

There was one bare patch, all else covered in snow.
What was that I saw? A robin, wouldn't you know?
They're supposed to be a harbinger of spring.
Which is hard to believe. I hadn't heard them sing.
I can guarantee, there are no insects there.
Earth worms have burrowed deep, their normal fare.
These are Canadian robins as claimed by more than one.
They migrate south maybe seeking the sun.
Robins are strict insectivores, or so I'd thought.
Then I saw several, dried berries they sought.
Birds that migrate, it's not warmth they seek,
But getting food when conditions become more bleak.
Bird feathers form excellent insulation.
However, can it withstand winter's tribulation?
These robins should fly another thousand miles down,

Where food and warmth are more readily found.
New England is not fertile winter ground.

4. The Robbing Robin

The rhododendron grew and grew and grew so well,
It covered the kitchen bow window after a spell.
We couldn't bear to trim it, such a noble bush.
The flowers bloomed so beautiful and lush.
During the cold months, it was like spring green,
Though the outside world couldn't be seen.
For the birds this was ideal for a nest,
Hidden from view from the crows and the rest.
A hard working thrush claimed the place
And constructed a thrush nest in the space.
Then a wonder, an aggressive robin chased the thrush.
It wanted a nest ready made though there was no rush.
Never mind that mud is what robins normally use
To help bind sticks and grass they'd carefully choose.
The robin couple raised their young right there.
I presume the thrush chose another spot with care.
The idea of not sticking with nature's plan surprised me so.
Also, I always thought robins were such wimps as birds go.
A little postscript is appropriate here.
We added to the house after a few years.
The rhododendron had to go since it was in the way.
One limb rested on the ground and rooted where it lay.
This I cut off, and I carefully planted it anew.
Son of rhoda prospered, and there it grew.
However, after 20 years few flowers bloom,
Maybe because passing deer too much consume.

5. Joe the Crow

When the summer was over, there was a great thing to do.
We'd visit an Audubon place. It was something like a zoo.
Only here they had farm animals to see.
Plus, a variety of wild ones who could no longer be free.
If you found an injured animal, you'd take it there.
It would be treated with tender loving care.
All the birds and a few mammals had their space.
Except for one. Joe the Crow had the run of the place.
Joe was deformed and small for a crow.
If he was injured, it was before he had time to grow.
Joe would wait for guests to come his way,
Then carefully sneak up, his method of play.
He'd untie shoelaces by pulling an end,
Then hop away chuckling. He'd made a new friend.
I know we shouldn't give animals human traits,
But Joe had a sense of humor. Don't berate.
You would swear he was laughing at his trick.
His victims certainly laughed and had a kick.
Poor Joe paid the penalty that goes with being free.
He was a carnivore's victim, the way nature meant it to be.
Countless people missed him including my family and me.

6. Playful Hawks

When you stop and smell the roses, you can't go wrong.
When you stop listening to noise. You hear nature's songs
Stop and look up from your tasks and see.
For a moment join nature and be free.
House work, the skillsaw whines across the land.
The hammer bangs. Every nail driven home by hand.
Stop and rest the arm, hawk whistles I hear.

I must look to see it, no to see them, so near.
Youth with energy, two siblings or mates,
Aerial combat, a game or type of date.
No need to practice. This must be play.
They don't catch their prey this way.
Soon they pass beyond the tall trees.
Unlimited sky for games in the breeze.
And I go back to my work, done with my ease.

7. Nature's Way

Our town has a quiet little pond, Fawn Lake by name.
No fishing, boating, swimming, skating or hunting for game.
Lake is rather pretentious considering its size.
Man made and four feet at its deepest on one side.
Walking around it makes a nice little outing for us,
The sloping lawn on one side is a plus,
Which attracts Canada geese, grass with water near.
Because of their droppings, geese bring no cheer.
They mate for life. They're noble and strong.
They can fly continuously, the distance long.
No rest and powered by a veggie diet,
They manage for twenty years to fly it.
Once we watched mom and dad goose with their brood.
A half dozen babies paddling along like they should.
In a blink one gosling disappeared from view.
The adults honked and flapped as we see them do.
This display had no effect on the terror from below,
A large snapping turtle had delivered the blow.
Nature is neither kindly or cruel in this ordeal.
Each species must eat to survive, no matter how we feel
Yet it saddens me when the young provide the meal.

8. Orioles

We had two weeping willows out front rather big.
I called them trash trees due to leaves and twigs.
The weeping parts broke off continuously, no lull.
Each year maybe 20 trash cans full.
They were buggy too. These landed on me
When mowing the lawn under those damn trees.
Baltimore orioles loved those bugs it seemed.
They built their nest, the location a dream.
This was a wonder constructed of woven straw,
Which formed a hanging pouch with nary a flaw.
It held the weight of adult and nestlings too,
And resisted falling when strong winds blew.
Orioles instinctively know how to construct this wonder.
I doubt most people could duplicate it without a blunder.
In the autumn one willow crashed in a hurricane squall
The other for no known reason decided to fall.
The latter broke the windshield of my car.
I was about to drive away and didn't get far.
Did nature somehow have it in for me,
Since I had no use for those trashy trees?
I do miss the colorful orioles who never came back.
Of desirable bugs other trees seem to lack.

9. Hard Working Wrens

We had a cheap swing set in our back yard.
The tops of the hollow legs were open except for a guard.
I noticed a wren disappear in that spot.
"He's building a nest like as not."
I'd read that males may select four nesting sites.
His intended mate picks the one that's just right.

What a tremendous amount of work to please a mate.
It's nature's intention. I hoped fatherhood turned out
great.
The couple brought twigs and grass, and the nest was
done.
Soon many trips brought insects for the young.
Later I spotted a baby who'd landed on the ground.
It was watched over 'til no longer earth bound.
I'm not sure how many young flew from the nest.
With their parents' devotion they were certainly blest.
A few years later I moved the swing set away
And learned what the wren did on the earlier day.
He had filled up the swing set leg. He didn't stop
Until the twigs and straw were up to the top.
I guess the wrens really know how to work.
Later we saw something that made me berserk.
A tiny wren was feeding this giant, a cow bird.
The story here is true, I give you my word.
The mother cow bird lays her eggs in other birds' nests.
The cow bird young will kick out the rest.
This is one evolutionary step that seems so wrong.
All species' young should stay where they belong.

10. Crow in Pursuit

Crows have been found to be rather smart birds.
They use tools and can even be taught a few words.
Most hear the caws and see the color black.
Due to these, some figure of compassion crows lack.
They are assigning human feeling to the crow,
Who are what they are as we all should know.
We've seen crows move from limb to limb,
Searching for bird nests, the result grim.

If you see a crow chased by song birds two,
Nobody is guarding the nest as one should do.
The second crow gets an easy meal that way.
It's nature's plan, which is what I hate to say.
Anyway, the song birds are like fighter planes in their attack,
While the crow is a bomber which can't fight back.
I've seen the reverse, crows attacking a hawk in flight.
Crows would normally be victims in a one-on-one fight.
They make sweeping passes like in aerial combat you'd see.
Actually, no one seems to get hurt in this type melee.

11. Adaptable Birds

Some species adapt to the presence of man.
Rodents come to mind though I'm thinking avian.
English sparrows and pigeons have adapted best.
They eat most anything. We provide sites for nests.
When I was a kid, one house had a hole in the wall.
Sparrows occupied it every year from spring to fall.
They'll nest in store signs or under the eaves.
I've never seen them in bushes or trees.
In cities pigeons seem to thrive the most.
Building ledges and bridge I-beams are the host.
Both these birds pick stuff from the ground,
Seeds, crumbs, insects, other detritus they've found.
People are unaware of a few other dependent birds.
Robins are all over, some lawns in herds.
Traditionally, barn swallows nest in buildings on farms.
They are dependant. In return they eat insects by the swarm.
Blue birds have found apple orchards are good places to

dwell.
Unfortunately, wormy apples don't sell too well.
The trees require spraying several times a year,
So blue birds are rare, the cause being clear.
When people poison their lawns, robins take the hit.
They're still around. Do people give a whit?
Living close to people has two sides you see.
Adapting is a wonder but not completely.

12. Camp Swallows

The unused farm was a common New England sight.
For a camp the buildings and fields were just right.
A dammed up stream made a nice swimming hole.
When mowed, athletic areas were the fields' role.
The barns and other buildings provided on the site
Were bunk houses, mess hall, activity space for day or night.
They kept a few farm animals for the kids' fun.
The farm experience was not known by everyone.
Swallows who'd shared space, remained where they were.
An extra little camp benefit, that's for sure.
Two swallows built their nest above the mess hall door.
Even though everyone passed six times or more.
Four little feathery heads would peek at the crowd.
Maybe wishing the kids were not so loud.
Mom and dad would wait 'til no one was in view
Before returning with insects to feed their hungry crew.
I loved that sight, hope all the kids did too.

13. Ospreys

Traveling near water down in southern lands,
We saw power line poles. On top some platforms stand.
It took but a second to determine why,
When we saw a large bird flying nearby.
These were placed for ospreys' nesting sites.
Unnatural, but for the birds, they were just right.
We saw the piles of sticks up there,
Not unlike eagles great building flair.
Once we were in a south Everglades parking lot.
I heard this scream in the sky, a small dot.
At the side of the pavement on a special pole,
A nest was sited, the naturalists goal.
I heard the scream again. Little heads popped up.
Dad was returning with food for them to sup.
In his talons he was carrying a large fish.
He was telling his kids to prepare for their dish.
You have wonderful experiences when you listen and see.
Of all in that park, this meant the most to me.

14. Turkey Courting

Many parts of town have wild turkeys wandering around.
We've had flocks of them on our lawn and grounds.
They scratch among leaves looking for bugs and seeds.
Usually, it's moms and the young they lead.
Once we had females and several males.
The toms raised their wings and feathers on their tails.
Their wattles hung down, to me an ugly sight.
Do these and their "beards' attract the hens? They might.
They strutted about sometimes stomping their feet.
Trying to impress each female they'd meet.

The females were oblivious. They could care less.
They continued searching for food, with them don't mess.
Maybe it's just for the other males, this showing their stuff.
They decide who's number one with bluster and bluff.
Better than fighting and dying when you've had enough.

15. Chasing Turkeys

"Can we chase the turkeys?" the granddaughters asked.
I thought for a second, for them it would be a blast.
There were maybe 20 of these, hens and their young.
What harm would we do? So the deed was done.
The hens flew straight up to trees and house tops.
The chicken size babies flew to bushes where they stopped.
So much for protecting the young, nature's law.
First take care of yourself against tooth and claw.
Apparently, the turkey species survives this way,
When a coyote, fisher cat or fox makes a play.
After mating the toms are nowhere to be seen.
Their aggression would help the flock. They are damn mean.
I'm surprised any babies survive when all's said and done.
They have to find their own food from day one.
They scratch around the leaf litter. It's a hard go
When the winter is harsh, the ground covered in snow.
Turkeys were introduced to Massachusetts in recent years,
And they have prospered as it appears.
Our granddaughters will always remember the day
When they chased the turkeys who flew away.

16. Baby Birds

Most birds take very good care of their young.
After hatching they stay where their lives had begun.
Dad and mom work their tails off bringing food.
It's a full time job taking care of their brood.
After the young have fledged, they leave the nest.
The parents continue feeding them without rest.
Now what's the difference with geese and ducks,
Chicken types and turkeys, the young have less luck.
They're expected to follow mom and see what she eats.
How do they know what's good? Will it be a treat?
How do their moms defend them? They can't fly.
When a predator shows up, I guess they die.
I wonder how any of these baby birds stay alive.
By nature, enough do such that each species survives.

17. Great Blue Herons

We were driving west on Route 2, a four lane road.
Not an interstate, but it carried a big traffic load.
We noticed a dozen cars parked on the other side.
Unusual, we couldn't figure why though we tried.
Hours later driving east, we came upon the spot.
Cars were still there, this time not a lot.
All the people were outside standing there.
We stopped to see what drew their stares.
It was a dismal swamp with several dead trees.
We looked up and saw in many of these
Large mounds of sticks piled up high.
These were nests. Soon a large bird flew by.
A great blue heron lit on its nest.
One small head popped up and then the rest.

More than a dozen nests were built there.
Great blues like nest sited high in the air.
People are entranced by nature it seems.
Stopping to observe satisfies one of our dreams.
We watched for awhile, parents returned with food.
I imagine it takes much effort feeding the brood.
A short time later we passed the site again.
No cars were stopped like there had been.
Then we saw the signs courtesy of the state.
"No parking or standing," the attraction was too great.
I read that great blues prefer locations like these,
Which gives them wing clearance between the trees.
A few years later we again passed that spot.
The dead trees had lost their limbs due to rot.
The great blues found another swamp like as not.

18. Intelligent Crows

Of all the birds, the most intelligent are crows.
Old timers from experience are in the know.
Grandpa said that when a crow sitting nearby
Saw someone approach, it knew to stay or fly.
He claimed crows could tell a gun from a stick.
A shotgun and it would fly off lickety split.
Grandpa waged a war. The crows ate planted seed corn.
Picking it from the ground by the following morn.
This was cured in a rather inventive way
By coating the seed with tar. What else in that day?
I've found that crows know how to get by.
Once I heard their racket. They covered the sky.
They congregated at this one spot in the woods.
I went to investigate. Were they up to no good?
The cause of their alarm, a barn owl perched on a limb.

The crows were making passes to torment him.
When I arrived, the owl proceeded to fly off.
More than 100 crows scrambled aloft.
I didn't think crows would be a barn owl's prey.
Obviously, the crows didn't feel that way.
With intelligent cooperation they ruined the owl's day.

19. The Invisible Boundary

Some birds get so used to man and his works.
You'd think they wouldn't act berserk.
Several times I've been on our porch reading a book,
When I'd hear a thump. Some bird didn't look.
He didn't see the screen flying down low,
Taking a short cut when he got the blow.
You would think that both glass and screen,
With birds superior eyesight would easily be seen.
Once I heard a banging on our French doors.
A robin was hitting the glass, what for.
I chased him away, thinking, "What a stupid bird."
He was back in a few minutes not being cured.
I pondered a minute and divined the reason why.
He could see his reflection, a rival had stopped by.
Figuring this poor creature wouldn't stop,
I had to find a solution before he dropped.
Taping a piece of cardboard on the inside of the glass
Stopped the aggressive robin's fruitless clash.
The alternative, sooner or later his brains he'd bash.

Chapter 4. Wonders of Lesser Species

The lesser beasties got my interest as a kid.
I watched insects, fish and reptiles. Glad I did.

1. Lesser Species

There's a poem here describing changes in 50 years.
I was thinking about megafauna including deer.
Then I thought of the little things, turtles, snakes, toads.
Once there were enough so they'd be squashed on the road.
At dusk in the summer, bats would fly about.
White nose disease puts their survival in doubt.
This explains the large change in one species,
But I wonder about the rest of these.
In ages past kids would find a box turtle in the yard.
They'd want to keep it and begged real hard.
Most parents would relent with one proviso.
In a few days they had to let the turtle go.
I haven't seen a box turtle in decades past.
The same with snakes and toads. Have I seen the last?
Hell, I used to have yellow jacket hives every year.
These too seem to have just disappeared.
Is something new in the environment we've all feared?

2. Yellow Jackets

Yellow jackets are our killer bees, native born.
They're aggressive, stinging repeatedly with their hellish thorn.
Minding my own business I've felt their ire.
Just moving an old fence post, my leg felt on fire.
Their nest was around the corner in the ground.
Vibrations must have seemed a threatening sound.
Standing on a ladder scrapping paint on the eaves,
An old man can move pretty fast you better believe.
In the attic yellow jackets had built their hive.
Scrapping said danger. I almost took a dive.
Tapping the swing set while mowing the lawn,
Resulted in yellow jackets charging in a swarm.
That time the swing set leg was the nesting site.
Anything that bugs them is sure to incite.
The worse attack was against our niece, age eight about.
She was playing in the bushes when they came out.
She ran to the house being stung all the way.
We put her in a cold bath, the pain to allay.
We were worried about induced shock from the pain.
The unfair attack upset her most in the main.
What surprised us, they were buzzing around the door
Waiting for her to come out to sting some more.
The devilishness of that behavior took me aback.
Was the hive mentality that intelligent in their attack?
Each time I managed to destroy their hives,
Pouring insecticide in the opening so none survived.
This is best done on a rainy type day.
Then the yellow jackets can't fly away.
A side note of interest, something we never knew.
They make their hives like paper wasps do.

On our front steps I noticed a bare spot.
A yellow jacket was pulling wood fibers. They'd removed a lot.
That's where the material for paper was gotten.

3. Spider Wonders

We can look with wonder at the lesser forms of life.
Surprising behavior among arachnids and insects is rife.
The lowly spider we may squash without a thought,
Has this tremendous ability of which most know naught.
Spinning a web is complicated, more than you'd realize.
Each web is different both in shape and size.
The spider can excrete several types of strand.
One type will stick wherever it lands,
Then dry so the spider won't get stuck.
Other strands remain sticky, for a fly bad luck.
When an insect gets caught, the spider responds.
With speed the victim is wrapped with unbreakable bonds.
At times a spider will move if its unpleased.
It will let out a strand, taken by the breeze.
If the strand catches, the spider can climb across.
Strand and spider can get air born. Crashing causes no loss.
Then for it's web, it will choose a new site.
In a few hours of hectic work all will be right.
We watched out for spiders in fields as kids.
Large yellow and black ones in the high grass were hid.
I did my share of teasing. Touch the web with a stick,
And watch the spider zip over unaware of my trick.
I've seen where eggs are laid in a sack,
And spotted the young on the web or mom's back.

As a kid I was fascinated by these things,
Which will always be wondrous. To me nature sings.

4. Deer Ticks

Growing up in New Jersey, I never saw a tick.
We played all the time in woods most thick.
Deer were ubiquitous with no hunting on public land.
I saw my first tick in eastern Maryland.
There each dog was free to roam, and he'd swim.
The salty bay water gave an advantage to him.
It discouraged the ticks except on his neck and head.
There, thumbnail size ticks attached and fed.
About 2007, I saw my first deer tick up north.
The deer population is way up of course.
The ticks like any mammal. I can't blame the deer.
I've had dozens attached ticks in recent years,
And treated four times for Lyme disease from these.
We've picked dozens off our dog found with ease.
Our dog has tick repellant and Lyme vaccine.
She's had no problem that the vet has seen.
I have read ticks can live a year without a meal.
They're inactive in winter. Cold's no big deal.
Deer walk on lawns and between each house.
Ticks are all over, maybe on every squirrel and mouse.
Should we stay inside and push to eliminate deer?
Or check ourselves daily with Lyme disease our fear?
I wonder, do wild animals get this disease? It's not clear.

5. Carpenter Ants

I've been observant since I was a kid long ago.
I noticed ants on the side of the house, oh no.
These were carpenter ants which tunnel through wood,
They will weaken a house. I knew they could.
For example, once while installing a pull down stair,
I removed three boards nailed together there.
All the soft part was removed from the center one.
They could be anywhere inside. What could be done?
My head is filled. I've read multitudes of thoughts.
Ants don't waste. Not everything needs to be caught.
If a member of the colony dies, he's consumed,
Same as any insect prey would be doomed.
I had saved some powdered poison, a type of DDT.
I powdered several ants before letting them go free.
After getting coated, they went on their way.
Either they made it or they were carried as prey.
An ant eats a poisoned ant and then it dies.
In turn it's eaten until to the colony we say goodbye.
With milligrams of poison I took care of the ants.
Better than fumigating, It's effectiveness not being by chance.
Overuse of DDT was bad though great at first glance.

6. Night Crawlers

We used earth worms for bait when we fished.
Kids didn't use lures. For big game fish we wished.
Maybe night crawlers would provide for our need.
With these giant earth worms we might succeed.
They came out of grassy ground on dewy nights.
Being up to ten inches long, they'll give girls a fright.

Armed with a flashlight, we searched the grass.
With these we might catch a pickerel or bass.
The worms are covered with light reflecting slime.
Easy to spot, you can catch them almost every time.
Sometimes they'd zip back into the ground.
They always kept their back end anchored we found.
When two were hitched together, they were easy to get.
As kids we didn't know much about sex yet.
However, night crawler reproduction is hard to forget.

7. Catfish

As kids we usually caught small panfish.
Catching the sport fish was our fervent wish.
We used earth worms for bait, not normal fish food.
The fish were attracted at least if in the mood.
We used corks to suspend the hook and bait.
If we guessed the depth wrong, results weren't so great.
Catfish stayed on the bottom where they fed.
Hooking one meant a problem which I would dread.
A cat has three rigid spines behind its gills.
To deter a predator, these certainly will.
To hold a cat, I knew the special way,
While removing the hook without ruining my day.
Once I caught this tiny, tiny little guy.
How did he get the hook in his mouth and why?
The reason for avoiding the spines, I found,
Much worse than a bee, the pain did truly astound.
I unhooked the little guy and let him go.
Not the cruel treatment given by other guys I know.
Better to catch and release unless used for food.
The baby fish swam back to its brood.

8. Sunfish

Sunfish, bluegill, or pumpkin seed, what's in a name?
They each describe one pan fish. They're all the same.
When we were kids, this was the most common caught.
Plus perch and catfish, of game fish there were naught.
Under water I knew a sunfish by the spot on its gill.
They are exceptional, and explain this I will.
You may see a clean spot near a pond's shore.
Of rotting vegetation or other debris there's no more.
This is a sunfish nest area, mom is there.
Moving fins and tail, she's cleaned it with care.
Other fish deposit eggs, they're fertilized, that's it.
Nothing more, the job's done, so they split.
The sunfish cares for her nest and is always on guard.
She'll attack any intruder, no foe too hard.
Dangle any object including a hook with no bait,
And for one sunfish, you've sealed its fate.
I never told my friends this easy way.
I've kept it in my mind if there ever is a day,
When I'm lost and starvation I must keep at bay.

9. Hop Toads

We walked up the old dirt road toward the pond in the woods.
I don't think any car would use it, the surface no good.
I saw movement and looked down at my feet.
There were dozens of tiny toads, not what I'd expect to meet.
Not much bigger than a house fly, where were they from?
Hundreds of feet to the nearest water, had they come?
I presume toads are all amphibians like frogs.

Maybe they didn't spend time as pollywogs.
In later years I found paying attention gives you a reward.
Like when I discovered toads had burrowed under old boards.
This was a quiet damp place to spend the day
'Til the dew wet the grass and the heat passed away.
Once we had gravel across part of our front yard
For trucks, delivering concrete wouldn't be too hard.
I saw a toad approaching this rough spot,
And wondered. Hopping would surely hurt a lot.
It didn't try it. The toad got up on legs four,
And awkwardly walked, no need to get sore.
I had never heard of a walking toad before.

10. Snake Ball

We love New England. It's great we settled here.
So many attractions are available and quite near.
One favorite is Plum Island, about an hour by car.
This is a bird sanctuary with marshes inside sand bars.
The east side is undeveloped, open ocean, no land beyond.
The waves are unmodulated by anything out on the pond.
It's a great place to take the kids on an early spring day.
We'd walk along the beach looking for shells on the way.
Not many people were out to crowd the scene.
We could commune with nature serene.
We decided to walk upon the dunes with care,
So as not to tread on vegetation growing there.
I heard a rustling in the brush nearby.
Looking in I was surprised by what I spied,
A writhing ball of snakes starting to spread.
I'd never before seen this, but about it I'd read.
These were hibernating garter snakes just coming to.

45

For a bit of warmth, sleeping in a ball is what they do.
Witnessing this wonder is rarely done,
But my family and I were the ones.
Fortunately, our kids didn't dream of the day.
It was not horrible to them in any way.

11. Turtle Baby

Pay attention to your senses, I always say.
You may be surprised by what comes your way.
We were walking through the nature preserve.
Grass rustling by the pond, I had to observe.
It was a tiny turtle, and on closer look-see,
Characteristics of a snapper were apparent to me.
I wondered what the small beast could find to eat.
Maybe insects and crawling things served as a treat.
How do these lesser species survive early life all alone?
When they hatch, they are completely on their own.
No parents to protect them or guide their way,
Teach them about predators or what's their prey.
Yet for each species, enough of them get by
To keep that kind going as eons fly.
I turned the little snapper back to the shore,
Knowing that he would become a fearsome carnivore.
I'm not going to interfere with nature on this score.

12. Mosquito Larvae

I was adding onto our house a few decades ago.
The concrete was all poured, but progress was slow.
I had the floor put in early with no structure overhead.
Not the normal order, I had reason I said.
We had this tremendous downpour to make my day.

A half foot of water on the basement floor lay.
There were other things to do, so I waited a week.
I would syphon the water, conditions not too bleak.
When I climbed down onto the basement floor,
I saw these tiny swimming things, a thousand or more.
Mosquitos had laid eggs, the larva had hatched.
My impromptu "mosquito farm" had raised quite a batch.
What the little varmints ate, I haven't a clue.
This was rain water on concrete, not much of a brew.
I set up my syphon, a water filled garden hose,
And emptied the basement, easy as it goes.
Problem solved 'til the next cloudburst arose.
Standing water attracts mosquitos, now I know.

12. Gypsy Moths

What's to wonder about gypsy moths, those pests.
If your area doesn't have them, you are blessed.
We had an epidemic about 30 years age.
Oaks are their favorite, other trees will take a blow.
A sure sign of infestation is green leaf litter on the ground.
The caterpillars chew this off, and it flutters down.
In a week or two they'll denude a 60 foot tree.
Then move on to the next, continuing their eating spree.
Listening on the porch, hearing them is no strain.
The caterpillar droppings sound like light falling rain.
The larva will spin a cocoon for the pupa stage.
Which morphs to the moth to propagate the rampage.
Fortunately, they have just one generation per year.
The trees grow a second set of leaves, nothing to fear.
Unless this ravaging takes place three years straight.
For trees so affected, no cure, it's just too late.
Barriers were tried on trunks, foil with axle grease.

Spray for small plants, squashing them for mental peace.
Birds don't seem to like them. Nothing much will work.
However, sometimes nature prevails when things go berserk.
It seems gypsy moths have their own deadly disease.
If you are lucky, this can save your trees.

14. Snake Handling

"Hey, Mike. There's a snake right over here.
It's not poisonous, so there's nothing to fear."
"That's neat. Do you think I could hold it?"
My six year old was adventurous, not afraid a bit.
With all my experience, I'd never picked up a snake.
I had seen the technique, precautions to take.
I explained all animals that have teeth can bite.
That's why you grab it by the neck just right.
Mike picked up the snake. It whipped all about,
And sprayed snake poop, a great defense no doubt.
He dropped it, not from fear but surprise.
We went indoors to clean up and tell the guys.
We learned a couple of things that day.
Critters can surprise you in different ways,
And watch out for both ends or you might pay.

Chapter 5. Plant Wonders

I wonder about all the life that's green.
Without it no other life would be seen.

1. Dominant Plants

We have a little patch by the edge of the woods.
It's the end of where a "rock" garden once stood.
Former owners had planted it. Stuff didn't survive.
With too much shade, I couldn't keep things alive.
When we bought the place, blue berries grew.
The kids picked the berries but only a few.
Another forest plant, ferns shared the plot.
Before I knew it, ferns all over, berries not.
Well, ferns have been around for eons, it's true.
I'd expect they'd dominate. That's what I "knew."
We brought some English ivy from my mom's home.
And planted it in the rock garden. It started to roam.
Then I noticed the ferns gone, just ivy there.
I never knew a plant could spread everywhere.
The ivy grew into the woods and climbed the trees.
However, some was killed by the cold winter breeze.
I had noticed myrtle left over from the past.
It spread widely, I was aghast.
Suddenly myrtle was dominant. For ivy goodbye.
This seemed strange since it doesn't grow high.
As you'd expect, this isn't this poem's end.
It seems lilies-of-the-valley is the latest trend.
The lilies grow in the woods and don't mind the shade.
Right now they're growing over our glade.
All this change each averaging a decade.

Will I still be here for nature's next escapade.

2. Who's Tough

One can see toughness in the strangest places.
It's found in people of course. You see it on their faces.
It's also true in the natural world. I'll relate what I saw.
The lowest form of life still obeys nature's law,
Which is to survive, overcome the odds, be tough.
Can you picture a new section of driveway thick enough,
Packed ground, three inches of black top will do.
The weight of a car wouldn't break through.
After the driveway had been in place for some weeks,
I noticed a circular crack that went deep.
The next day a cone shaped piece had pushed up.
What phenomena had caused this to erupt.
I picked off the piece, and what was I seeing.
A rather large mushroom had sprung into being.
From such a simple life form, what could be the source?
Punching a hole in my driveway took one hell of a force.
I haven't filled it in. I want to show it of course.

3. The Survival Tree

The great towers had crashed to the ground.
Of the occupants only bits and pieces were found.
The cleanup crews were careful with open eyes.
They didn't want to let anything get by.
Removing two blocks of concrete, they spotted the tree.
With bark missing and broken limbs, they set it free.
The workers were about to consign it to the trash.
Their foreman said, "Stop, let's not be too fast.
The city has a plant nursery. I'll take it there.

I think we can save it with tender loving care."
The foreman himself had learned about survival.
He had faced death. Willpower postponed its arrival.
He covered the wounds. Given nutrients, water and sun,
The tree prospered until reconstruction was begun.
Some said this tree was the wrong type to replant,
But the foreman prevailed. He wouldn't accept the word can't.
A symbol to all of the determination to live,
The survival tree has this contribution to give.

4. The Will to Live

Some trees have light seeds they cast to the breeze.
They travel afar and land where they please.
This may be a dry wasteland or fertile ground,
Or a crack between rocks where some soil's found.
If it stays moist there, the seed will sprout.
Soon a young tree will poke its top out.
There's a lack of nutrients, so development is slow.
Such a tree is nature's Bonsai naturally grown.
They'll survive. People wonder how they make out.
Only one thing will kill them, a long term drought.
These trees can be found on mountainous terrain,
Where in general life is hard to maintain.
Once on a mountain hike we found a large rock.
It was standing alone like a giant kid's block.
It had ten foot vertical sides, a tree growing on top.
Over the decades down the sides roots had dropped.
A miracle had provided for the tree's need
Until its roots reached the ground beneath.
We've had the wonder in the gutters of our home.
Maple seeds like little helicopters were wind blown.

Leaf litter collects. It acts like soil you see.
Many seeds sprouted into a forest of tiny trees.
I'm heartless I guess and cleaned them out.
They should find another place to sprout.
One neighbor didn't notice, and so they grew.
A couple reached three feet before he knew.

5. The Great Wave

What a job. The paper wants a report from the scene.
There's total devastation. The ground is scrubbed clean.
Well, not clean. That's the wrong way to describe it.
Not a man made object stands. All's smashed to bits.
The rescue workers are moving through the debris.
Their first pass is to find anyone they can see.
It's quiet. Maybe they'll hear some survivor's voice.
Better to find those conscious given the choice.
I think they'll find thousands are missing or dead.
Some are buried, some swept to sea, both we dread.
Most of the vegetation was uprooted and carried away.
The tsunami's power is unbelievable. It's all I can say.
Here's a lone man looking through the debris.
If I talk to him, I hope he will not think ill of me.
My Japanese is good. I hope he understands.
"Sir, can I help you search, maybe clear some of the land."
"This is where my home stood. There's nothing left.
My family's gone, parents, wife, children. I'm truly bereft."
"I'm so sorry. Your whole family? How will you be?"
"Life goes on. Consider the single cherry blossom on that tree."
How many of us in our agony could so clearly see?

6. Mending Trees

The burning bush is supposed to be an invasive type.
Meaning it's not native and prospers, thus the hype.
We have several. They're well shaped and durable.
One was crushed by a truck, the damage curable.
There are several daughter plants bounding the woods.
They don't survive in the deep shade which is good.
I'm not concerned they'll crowd out native plants.
From experience the burning bush doesn't have a chance.
One of our bushes split in half with a heavy snow.
The ten foot beauty, we just wouldn't let it go.
So I tied it and bound it and braced both sides.
It grew back together and remained our pride.
Mending this bush gave me practice for a tree.
A young maple cracked and split, a challenge for me.
Before coming to our feeder, birds would alight there.
Checking out the surroundings with diligent care.
"Please save it," my concerned wife pled.
"I'll give it a shot, though it seems dead."
I propped up the tree having practiced before,
And wonder of wonders it was restored.
The maple prospered for a few years more.
'Til the next heavy snow. We knew what was in store.
This time it shattered with no possible repair.
Birds are adaptable, they don't need to alight there.
They still approach the feeder with care.

7. Roof Growth

Ever wonder what conditions are the most extreme
For plants to survive. It's worse than you'd dream.
The shingled roof on a typical house is the one.

It's hot enough to fry an egg in the direct sun.
The roof's like the Sahara except for rainy days.
Or cool nights bring a bit of dew its way.
In time patches of lichen will grow here and there.
More in the partial shade from the sun's glare.
There is no soil, maybe just dust from the air.
Yet life clings to the arid desert up there.
I've even seen green moss that dries out.
Then returns when dampness reverses the drought.
I've thought of power washing the lichen away,
But what the hell, their persistence wins the day.
They don't seem to damage the shingles in any way.

8. Rose Bushes

When we moved to our house decades ago,
A rail fence out front was mostly for show.
Former owners had planted beautiful roses there.
We tried to maintain them with tender loving care.
The rose stalks had a life cycle of three years.
A stalk would grow, no flowers would appear.
The second season there'd be a profusion of blooms.
With less the third year, then it would be doomed.
The dead heads and stalks, I always cut away,
Though this didn't affect the plants I'd say.
I had an aversion to poison with a dog and kids,
So I never helped these roses, the pests to rid.
No Japanese beetles but the roses were stripped clean
Several years when the gypsy moths arrived on the scene.
I hated the loss, but the roses died off.
Then a few years later a miracle, don't scoff.
Two bushes sprouted from remnants of two roots.
One is a bush, the other just a shoot.

We had transplanted a rhododendron on that spot.
Seeking sun the rose grew a lot.
No roses but for determination I give it a shot.

9. Save That Tree

The ice storm weighed down the tree and took a toll.
Uprooting half the arborvitae's boll.
I am the eternal optimist. I'd give it a try.
Some way I can jack it toward the sky.
Being next to the house, roots only half held it down.
This was to my advantage, I soon found.
I bought a "come-along" for which I had need.
With a hook on the house I knew I'd succeed.
A cable attached the house to the tree,
I gradually pulled it vertical you see.
I covered the exposed roots with some dirt,
And roped tree to house. It wouldn't hurt.
The arborvitae prospered from that date.
It's a foot in diameter and 30 feet high of late,
And after four decades it looks great.
A side benefit for a rather adventurous youth,
It provided him the means to climb onto the roof.

10. Save That Bush

"Grandpa, Mom says you're going to build a garage.
I don't want you to make the house too large.
Those two bushes are in the way.
They'll have to be cut. That's what they say.
That makes me sad. What can we do?"
What if your granddaughter asked you?
One's an arborvitae, and its roots go deep.

No way can I move it, but a promise I'd keep.
"After we build the garage, I will plant two more,
One on each side to bracket the door.
I will try to move the rhododendron there.
It won't be easy, but I'll take care."
Rhododendrons have shallow roots, so my chances were
good.
I got it out of the ground as I knew I would.
It was a heavy sucker, so I put down planks,
On which I slid the bush down a slight bank.
I got it in place quickly, so the roots wouldn't dry,
And built a stone wall, for level ground is why.
Then came the real work for six months more,
I drenched the bush daily, root growth to restore.
I satisfied my promise as my granddaughter implored.
The two new arborvitae are now eight feet,
And the rhododendron has prospered, the annual flowers
sweet.

Chapter 6. Natural and Man Made Wonders

Many must travel to Europe for wonders man made.
I prefer our natural wonders that won't fade.

1. Look to the Sky

I had a window office at work back in the day.
When necessary "to rest my eyes," looking out was the way.
I'd see that the great expanse of the midday sky.
It's surprising what was there as time passed by.
I noticed two cloud layers at different heights.
One moving east, one west, no trick of light.
I noticed contrails left by jet planes.
Their length determined by the air humidity. I'll explain.
Long contrails mean the air humidity is high.
On the other hand, short ones say it's dry.
I've seen a jet leave a trail through the clouds.
Hot engine exhaust thins the droplet crowds.
Most everyone has seen a rainbow after a storm.
Amid the clouds I've seen the colors in an arc form.
Rain isn't necessary. Varying refraction will do.
Scientific explanations should suffice for you.
Once on an interstate a double rainbow appeared.
People pulled over so their view would be clear.
I've watched clouds over mountains on a mostly clear day.
They'd disperse as they moved away.
When currents pass over obstacles, waves form in the air.
At the crests, air cools and clouds form there.

The part of the wave on the downward track
Warms and the cloud evaporates back.
How far can you see on a really clear day?
I found out in the west while driving away.
Arizona's Mt. Humphry was visible for 125 miles maybe more.
If we had gone farther, I could've raised the score.
The rarest phenomena I saw in the sky
Was a double sun. Maybe I can explain why.
Light rays from the sun transmitted directly to me.
Others aimed elsewhere were refracted so I could see.
I was in a parking lot, no one else was aware.
I felt lucky I saw the false sun up there.

2. The Grand Canyon

If you plan to travel, fly to the southwest.
Of all the natural wonders, the Grand Canyon is best.
The power of erosion over millions of years past
Has left this immense work. It will leave you aghast.
When we first saw it, we could just stand and gaze.
The grandeur is beyond my ability to praise.
The Colorado River now is a mile down.
Rock is still eroding, the water muddy brown.
At every point the canyon top is miles wide.
All the pyramids could be tucked out of sight inside.
We visited there in January, a great time to go.
It was warm enough, though there had been snow.
Since few people visit that time of year,
We could drive in, roads and parking lots clear.
Normally, shuttle buses carry all the crowds.
When there are so many people, no cars are allowed.
We stayed in a cabin, a picture window for view.

A fireplace provided atmosphere, a bit of warmth too.
You could also stay in the rustic lodge near there.
If you want excellent meals on your visit, that's where.
We were able to see the easternmost of the park
To the farthest west with sunset before dark.
Our cabin was at the head of Bright Angel Trail
Which is the path to the bottom. It has no rails.
We didn't consider this trek. You ride on mules.
I'm too old and well beyond the weight limit rules.
The canyon ought to be visited while you are young,
To make the trek and the rapids rafting run.
Everyone should see the Canyon. Put it on your list,
Of the great natural wonders not to be missed.

3. Yosemite Valley

Yosemite, called one of the prettiest valleys of all,
Is graced with four spectacular waterfalls.
This national treasure is in the Sierra Nevada Range.
The valley is at a high elevation which may seem strange.
This means enough water, in a state that's dry,
To support evergreen forests and lush grass nearby.
We visited Yosemite in May, the right time of year.
One road had just opened, the snow being cleared.
The flooding Yosemite River was back in its banks.
Everything was open. To Providence we gave thanks.
We drove up the length of Glacier Point road,
And saw 15foot piles from when it had snowed.
What a spectacular view, of four falls you could see three,
Vertical rock faces, water cascading down free.
The flat faced Half Dome was off to the right.
Past glaciers had ground it smooth, what might!
El Capitan, a monolith which means single stone,

Stood to the left, in the world the largest known.
I could stand there and look all day,
But it was time to leave and get on our way.
We had been going to camp, but due to the flood,
We stayed in the motel avoiding dampness and mud.
Reservations are usually needed for the lodge most grand.
The rustic construction fits nicely on this land.
Here you park your car and use the shuttle bus,
Which circles around the valley. You stop where you must.
We walked to the base of the famous Yosemite Falls,
Of the world's waterfalls, the second most tall.
Spectacular, noisy and quite damp, due to the spray.
We made it across the base on a slippery walkway.
We stopped at the museum where a historical film was shown,
Toured an Indian camp, authentic as well as known,
Then hiked to Bridal Vail Falls along a watery path.
Too much snow the prior winter, this the aftermath.
What a great experience, but I had some remorse.
If we were youths, we could hike to the falls source,
Or even try rock climbing in due course.

4. Yellowstone Park

When visiting Yellowstone, a great way is from the south.
You see the Grand Tetons. They'll leave an open mouth.
There's a flat expanse named Jackson Hole.
The mountains rise up abruptly, bless my soul.
In the post colonial era French trappers explored here.
Their name for the mountains, "Big Boobs" is clear.
We visited a Native American museum along the way,
Displaying artistic bead work from an earlier day.
The road rises to higher elevations in the park.

Waterfalls, spectacular vistas, don't drive it in the dark.
Soon you'll see Yellowstone Lake on the right.
This is an extinct volcanic crater. Imagine it's might.
In fact Yellowstone is located above a spot
Which due to geologic reasons is exceedingly hot.
Thus, the quantity of geysers and hot springs here.
Some 10,000, more than any other spot on our sphere.
Visit the lodge, a good place to have a meal.
Time it right and watch Old Faithful spout for real.
We stopped to see hot springs boiling away.
Then had to leave having had a long day.
We saw bison and elk by the herd.
Wolves are about their extinction cured.
When early Yellowstone explorers said what they'd seen,
People wouldn't believe, thinking it was a pipe dream.
On further exploration, the stories were found true.
To protect this wonder, it became a park in 1872.
The first national park world wide when new.
I've briefly described what we saw in a day.
Visit here and spend more time on the way.

5. General Sherman

Sherman was a union general in the Civil War.
That's where he earned his fame, but there's more.
Several of his soldiers joined an exploration party out west.
They tramped through the Sierra Nevada in their quest.
While exploring the land of the giant sequoia tree,
They found the largest living thing you'll ever see.
Thirty six feet in diameter, truly a wonderful sight.
They named it for Sherman as you'd expect they might.
The Sherman Sequoia is one of thousands of great trees.

A national park protects the best of these.
Visiting there is a must for any California trip,
With a motel, restaurants and visitor centers you shouldn't
skip.
The sequoias are second to coastal redwoods in height.
They stop at 300ft due to nature's might.
Lightning strikes sooner or later burn out their tops.
They continue to grow in diameter. Vertical growth stops.
Sequoias require specific conditions to grow.
The right altitude, rainfall, and temperature just so.
That's why they only grow where they do.
I'd try to extend their range, wouldn't you?
Sequoia has another unique property. You may have heard.
It has the five vowels, the shortest such English word.

6. Mount Rushmore

If you travel to South Dakota by bus or car,
Take in Deadwood from which Mt. Rushmore isn't far.
The drive from the east gives a neat view.
From within a tunnel the monument is framed for you.
This road has a feature about which I never knew.
For steep slopes there's pigtail turns, more than a few.
You go over a bridge, then go under that bridge on a
curve.
This reduces the slope, also space is conserves.
The monument is awe inspiring when you see it near.
Four great busts of presidents we hold dear.
Washington, the father of our country, our first.
Lincoln saved the Union which slavery had cursed.
Jefferson, the Declaration of Independence author.
Teddy Roosevelt who pushed for our world power.
All sculpted over 14 years ending in '41.

During the Coolidge presidency, it was begun.
The sculptor's name was Borglum, head of a crew.
They blasted rock with dynamite 'til they were through.
They removed 500,000 tons of rock. Now you know.
It was back breaking work to make it just so.
In later years, some wanted to add presidents of note.
Reagan, Kennedy, and Franklin Roosevelt got the vote.
Mt. Rushmore is a monument. Please let it stand.
If someone wants another, choose some other land.

7. Hoover Dam

If you visit the Las Vegas area, consider this.
Take a drive to Hoover Dam. You shouldn't miss.
It's not a natural wonder, that's agreed,
But the canyon is and so is Lake Meade.
Damming the Colorado River, it's a monument to man.
An example of the American spirit, I think I can.
For years this was the largest concrete structure on earth.
Just the wonder of looking down shows its worth.
Until recently the dam acted as an east, west road.
Now a great arched bridge takes the traffic load.
Originally, the dam generated power and controlled flooding.
Now it provides water where population is budding.
Very little of the Colorado makes it to the sea.
Thus, now the great turbines mostly set idly.
Construction of the Hoover Dam was started in '31.
The Great Depression was raging when begun.
The influential wanted to do great things.
Give people jobs and hope. These prosperity brings.
The building was not an easy task to do.
Tunnels were drilled for the river to run through.

A smaller dam was built to keep the site dry.
With the rock removal and construction five years went by.
As concrete dries and cures it generates heat,
So coolant pipes were imbedded in the concrete.
They called this the Boulder Dam for a time.
Many felt to name it after President Hoover was a crime.

8. Zion National Park

Utah has spectacular monuments and parks to see.
We visited two in the southwest country.
Utah was settled by Mormons in 1847.
For these persecuted people it was like heaven.
They were explorers looking for fertile land,
Since with time their numbers began to expand.
When they entered the Virgin River valley, they saw
Sculpted mountains rising up, inspiring awe.
Being religious people, the Mormons named things.
The mountains were the patriarchs, a religious ring.
Temple, Virgin River, and Angel Landing are there.
Names fitting the spectacular, chosen with care.
You drive through a mile long tunnel entering from the east.
Half way through there's a lookout, for the eyes a feast.
From this hole in the vertical rock wall,
You get a view of the river valley and mountains tall.
Then comes the road to the valley below.
With several hairpin turns, easy as she goes.
I swear at each turn, the bus front was over the side.
Except for our height, it was an amusement park ride.
All visitors park in the lot, bus and car.
Propane powered buses take you near and far.

There are visitor centers, an Omni theater, places to eat.
Still the wonder of it all can't be beat.
Walking trails are up high and rock climbing too.
If you're young and strong there's adventure for you.
Continue up the canyon on the river "side" trail.
Though part is under water with no guide rail.
Oh, to be young again, but age must prevail.

9. Bryce Canyon

Ebenezer Bryce discovered the canyon that bears his name.
A Mormon rancher, grazing land was why he came.
He described the locale, and it's still true now.
"It's a hell of a place to lose a cow."
Actually, Bryce isn't a canyon type landscape,
But a series of amphitheaters, horseshoe shaped.
Erosion over the millennia has done its work,
Leaving wonderous labyrinths that seems berserk
There are intricate ravines and columns tall.
These structures are "hoodoos." You'd think they'd fall.
Multi-colored limestone is the rock type.
Iron and manganese oxide layers provide layered stripes.
The best views are from roads above.
Though wandering about below is something I'd love.
Nearby are isolated structures of note.
The Salt and Pepper Shakers get my vote.
For awesome natural beauty go see Bryce.
For your time and money it's worth the price.

10. Oak Creek Canyon

When you travel to Arizona, Flagstaff's a good spot.
It's centrally located, for tourists there's a lot.
We don't make fixed plans except where we'll stay.
There may be more or less time along the way.
We had a few hours there late in the day,
So we visited Oak Creek Canyon south of there.
This is a state park about which I'll share.
We stopped at a parking lot with a vista to see.
The canyon stretched out beckoning to me.
Then I looked down and saw the winding road.
We were going to drive that? Yes at a speed slowed.
We saw rock formations like at Bryce.
Not as grand, but its hoodoos would suffice.
Walking trails beckoned plus the picnic grounds.
Except for a few picnickers, not many people around.
We sat by a meandering fast moving stream.
A pleasant interlude, beauty, calmness, a dream.
Too soon the sun dipped in the west.
To avoid driving the hairpins in the dark, no more rest.
For the nearby Sedona, wait for our next quest.

11. The Canadian Rockies

Fly to Calgary, a pleasant city on the western plains.
Then head west to the Rocky Mountain range.
Of Alberta Province this is the western most part.
The Rocky's ridge line is where British Columbia starts.
You enter the Banff National Park on the Trans-Canada highway.
Take the Banff ski lift, an aerial skyway.
From the top you have this spectacular view

Of the town of Banff with a river running through.
The surrounding mountains are bare rock.
Strata show the terrain raising in great blocks.
Banff has museums, cafes and a grand old hotel
More classy than our lodging in a modern motel.
Heading north Lake Louise requires a stop.
Of the prettiest lakes in the world it's the top.
At the far end a glacier is in full view.
A grand hotel provides luxury for you.
Farther north the Ice Field Parkway is our road
With sparkling mountain tops on which it recently snowed.
We stopped for a meal, cafeteria style.
Then rode to the Athabasca glacier, only a few miles.
We rode up on the ice in a radically altered bus.
Giant wheels and slow speed made it safe for us.
We dismounted on the glacier and walked about.
Glacier ice is different. It tasted the same I found out.
The Columbia Ice Field is the largest in the west.
Covering 100 square miles, up to 3000 feet thick, it's the best.
Along the highway, there are lookouts to see.
The most beautiful mountains we all agree.
At one stop we couldn't leave the bus.
A recently wakened bear might be an ornery cuss.
There are train rides through this wonderful terrain.
At my age on the bucket list this will remain.

Chapter 7. Scientific Wonders

There are so many wonders around us to see.
Understanding part of it makes it more wonderful to me.

1. The 20th Century's Greatest Discovery

Back in the days of Newton, Galileo, and their kin,
They considered the state that science was in.
The result: all the important problems were solved,
The discovery of gravity and how the heavens were involved.
They could explain planetary motion about the sun.
This had concerned astronomers since time had begun.
I shouldn't belittle the great men of the past.
If they had a hint about the future, they'd be aghast.
This lack of imagination has appeared at other dates.
Like the railroad, can anything travel at a faster rate?
The telegraph meant communication over distances wide.
No thought of improvement until radio arrived.
With time discoveries were made at faster rates.
Nobody can predict the direction, they'll take.
Of last century's discoveries which was the most great?
Some say the transistor, the best we can create.
However, the very greatest discovery by far,
Finding how much we don't know gets the star.
What wonders await us as the future unwinds.
We'll just have to wait to see what we find.

2. Totally Clear Night

Sometimes I wish I lived farther from city lights
Which completely mess up seeing stars on a clear night.
It seems all is against my having a nice view.
I can hardly see the Big Dipper, Polaris too.
It's mostly light pollution, but also there's misty sky.
Both seem to get worse as time flows by.
I do know conditions improve in Winter's cold.
Maybe it's Canadian air, it's drier I've been told.
I look forward to two brief vacations each year.
Both are far from any city, and the air is clear.
Well after sundown, we can go down to the dock,
Lay out on the deck chairs and forget the clock.
The Milky Way is obvious arching across the sky.
The center of our galaxy where billions of stars lie.
Our nearest neighbor is four light years away.
The firmament is so vast, can I comprehend it this way?
I remember the 50-50 rule for the nearest star.
50,000 years, traveling at 50,000 mph to go that far.
If we're lucky, we will see a meteor flash by,
Maybe one second before it burns and dies.
Then there are the satellites. The first caused a stir.
The papers printed times and where one would appear.
Now it's a matter of chance, if you happen to see.
Brighter than Venus, Skylab is reported to be.
You can see stars down to the horizon on clearest nights.
With hilly terrain they move. It's refracted light.
This is due to varying density of the air
Which is moving over the hills out there.
One phenomena I'm still waiting to see,
Northern lights, on my bucket list it'll remain to be.

3. Evolution-transition

Evolution explains a lot about animals over the years.
With time there are changes, new species appear.
There were fish, then later breathers of air.
Many examples of species in between are there.
Like fish that spend time out of water, we find
Mud skippers and walking catfish come to mind.
The next step, species hatched in water have gills.
These grow up with lungs filling the bill.
Some amphibians need to stay damp like frogs.
Toads' skin can be dry. They stay clear of the bogs.
Dinosaurs and reptiles from the water are rid,
Though they lay eggs like their forebears did.
Some of the transitional species still are here,
Or they left fossils records, their existence clear.
There are very specialized animals like the bat.
How could a transitional animal get like that?
With half developed wings you can't fly.
On the ground they're a detriment. You can't get by.
Now there's the naked ape, a descriptor of man.
How did we change? From gatherer of what we can
To inventor, to thinker, to word speaker,
To writer of stories and truth seeker.

4. Atoms to Atoms

The minister intones, "Ashes to ashes and dust to dust."
It's traditional. To say these words is a must.
The message here is nature's recycling of all.
We're consumed by bacteria, fungi, and other things small.
The Hindus are right about the fact we'll endure.

Maybe not our consciousness but our substance for sure.
Rather than dust, consider we're composed of atoms instead.
All are ready for reuse when we're dead.
Hydrogen is the most common due to our water content.
Here lies a theoretical result about which I'll comment.
All hydrogen in the universe was created 14 billion years ago
Shortly after the big bang made it so.
We're also composed of oxygen, carbon, calcium and more.
These are atoms created in star cores.
When early stars went nova large atoms went free
And seeded the universe for the likes of you and me.
All the atoms of life are billions of years old.
If they could tell us, what stories would be told.
Some of our atoms have been in millions of things
From single cell animals to the jungle kings.
Dinosaurs, mud worms, snakes and trees,
Ancient ferns, flowers and fruit, birds and bees.
Maybe for interpreting the gospel, this is the way.
Recycling atoms is life everlasting to the end of days.
If you consider all the atoms here and in space,
Only a tiny fraction are involved in life in our place.
How significant are we of the human race?

5. Dimensional Analysis

There's a science technique about which few are aware.
It's called dimensional analysis, words sure to scare.
Probably you will say, "That's enough for me.
This science stuff is baffling as you can see."
Just think of dimensions like feet and pounds.

It's how we put numbers on all that's around.
For analysis, think analyze or study of some thing.
We reap the benefit that understanding brings.
Applying it to animals, nature can't violate the law.
There are size limits from conclusions we draw.
All animals need oxygen. Think invertebrate and their kin.
They absorb what's needed through pores in their skin.
Their need is proportional to their weight,
While surface area determines oxygen supply rate.
So insects, molluscs, and worms have size limits and always will,
Unless like the octopus they develop some type gill.
Another example is the limit on birds' size.
Lift is proportional to wing area. It's how one flies.
So no giant bird, the roc from Sinbad fame.
No glued feathered flight. That was Icarus's game.
Also, no animal too large beyond sauropod and whale.
Hummingbird and shrew are limits, smaller ones fail.
Wait a minute, how about ancient roaches and dragon flies,
Not to mention pterodactyls, four times a condors size?
Explanation: back then the air was much more dense.
Skin pore breathing and big wing span made sense.
Who'd think biology could be analyzed with math?
What wonders the human mind constructs along our path.

6. Complete the Family Tree

A nephew did a genealogy study of our family tree.
It was complete through four generations up to me.
That's thirty people for whom we have names,
Plus birth dates and places from where they came.

It would be neat to know the rest of the story,
Like all children's names, occupations, any fame or glory,
And their age at death and also the cause.
Were they decent people or crooks breaking the laws?
But alas, the records don't tell us much.
There are no stories for bragging rights and such.
I started thinking about what would be fun.
Keep track of all genealogy searches done.
These data could be entered in a massive computer file.
You could find information in a short while.
Names of remote aunts and uncles could be proved.
Plus cousins who are many times removed.
Then instead of a direct family tree,
I'd have a family tangle related to me.
With the computer keeping track of people known,
There'd be so much data my mind would be blown.
With the wonder of computers we could keep track,
Or else it would be a horror. Think of an attack
By an unknown relative who wouldn't get off my back.

7. The Sun

Ah, what a wondrous thing, this star, our sun.
Rain is necessary, but a sunny day's more fun.
When sunlight is limited, people often get depressed.
The cure, exposure to bright light is stressed.
Primitive people worshiped the sun as a god.
Knowing all life depended on it, not so odd.
Northern people prayed through winter's cold,
The sun's warmth would return breaking the icy hold.
The primitives were right. Life depends on the sun.
Conditions not just so, life wouldn't have begun.
The light and heat we get is from nuclear fire,

Occurring at the proper rate or the sun expires.
Too slow and our sun would be too dim.
Too fast, a super nova makes life's chances slim.
Our sun has burned steadily for billions of years,
And here we are, for our wondrous sun give cheers.

8. Speculation

I read a lot of articles of a scientific bent.
These are written so you can understand what's meant.
Real scientific articles appear in journals read by few.
Those I read give me but a layman's view.
There's a tremendous amount of speculation here.
Things that can't be verified in a way that's clear.
Some describe what happened many years ago.
Stuff that the fossil record can't possibly show.
Dinosaurs were warm blooded and had feathers like birds.
They took care of their young and traveled in herds.
Maybe this is all true, though there are slips.
I prefer to think they're reptiles with different hips.
They speculate on how evolution has worked.
Life is so complicated, it can make you go berserk.
Theories are good when evidence verifies their worth.
Theories based upon theories have an illegitimate birth.
Then there are the proposals about what might be done.
Where anything is possible under the sun.
The space elevator, feeding the world's masses,
Curing cancer, ways out of the global warming morass.
If you have a wild idea, write a paragraph or two.
A full size article is too much for what you'd like to do.
This world is a complex wonderful place you see.
Don't burden us with theories on what you think should be.

9. Sense of Smell

Our noses certainly provide us with pleasure.
The odor of carnations and roses are a treasure.
Aromas also heighten our sense of taste.
A stuffed up nose, and eating seems a waste.
Countless odors too faint to detect are out there.
They pass with the wind, each of us unaware.
Man's companion through the ages is another case.
Dogs can detect odors so faint, there's but a trace.
When I walk my dog, she's so anxious to go out.
It's her john, but also there's new odors about.
She'll smell a trail, but sometimes a thin stick.
She studies it. Maybe for remembrance it's the trick.
I've wondered how many molecules were left here
By some other dog, raccoon, cat or deer.
How many molecules are emitted available to smell?
I think but a tiny amount and yet my dog can tell.
Perhaps dogs learn to choose odors to pay attention to.
Else they'd overload their brains like some people do.
People learn to ignore the constant auditory stew.

10. Our Autumn

Ah, it's autumn, my favorite time of year.
I love the cool air, though winter is near.
It means I can do honest labor without excess sweat,
Cutting and splitting wood not getting soaking wet.
I like raking leaves and toting them out back.
Most of my neighbors must think that I'm daft.
All the trees are getting ready for winter's sleep.
The little rodents collect seeds and nuts to keep.
The colors are dazzling. We don't need to travel north.

We are blessed by the variety of hues coming forth.
The brightest yellow comes from Norway maples,
Though the red maple is the foliage staple.
We have a profusion of burning bushes here.
For their full color, of shade they must be clear.
Ours turn a light pink with some leaves just white,
Not the brilliant crimson, but that's all right.
Our two Japanese maples provide the bright red,
That flash before they sleep like the dead.
Yet we're surrounded by evergreens, their worth,
Is to remind us of the promise of spring's rebirth.

11. Sun Rise and Set

Sunup, sundown, sunup, sundown, swiftly flow the days.
How do we measure time's passage? This is the way.
Unfortunately, we've lived where these can't be seen.
With hills and trees and buildings in between.
We spent our honeymoon at Florida's Miami Beach.
Somehow, the thought of sunup wasn't in our reach.
Years later while visiting Cape Canaveral there,
I remembered about sunup and the day was fair.
I walked to the beach at the start of day.
Then, damn it, there was too much haze.
Oddly, I met a coworker with the same idea.
Well, we got a good view of the early morning sea.
We visited the Grand Canyon in recent years.
Again, the mist was too thick as I had feared.
We were on a family trip to the Florida west coast.
Everyone wanted to see the sun setting the most.
This time we got to the beach just in time
To see the golden orb sink into the brine.
We didn't see the green flash in the western sky

Which is reportedly fairly rare to spy.
At home we get an occasional spectacular sunset.
In the autumn in New England they're a good bet.
One day we'll see the sun rising from the sea.
Cadillac Mountain at Bar Harbor, Maine is good for me.
This is where it's first seen in the USA.
It's on my bucket list where it'll probably stay,
Since with my luck it will be cloudy on the planned day.

12. Thank God for Gravity

Nobody can really say why gravity is here.
Mass attracts mass. This fact is quite clear.
Physicists call it a force that's weak.
It's just right, otherwise life would be bleak.
Too little gravity, we'd lose our water and air.
No small planet can support life out there.
Too much gravity and we'd weigh a ton.
Large animals would have to crawl and never run.
Perhaps only the water could support large life.
On land maybe only short plants and bugs would be rife.
If an intelligent species developed in such a place,
Life would be extremely hard for this race.
No animal help with leather, wool, fur and meat.
No beast of burden for prodigious labor feats.
No trees big enough for lumber to build
Needed structures with this species to be filled.
Everyone knows things fall. It's plane to see.
The concept of gravity was Isaac Newton's idea.
Where there is mass, gravity will always be.

Chapter 8. Wonders of Ancient Man

Evidence indicates that great apes are our kin.
How wonderful, we progressed to the state we're in.

1. Abstract Thought

When did ancient man start abstract thought?
We don't think animals do it though some can be taught.
The meaning of certain words our dog knows.
She'll race to the door if I mention walk, out or go.
Even pigeons can learn to count in a rudimentary way.
If they peck correct numbers, they get corn for pay.
Is this abstract, associating a word with an act?
The pigeon doesn't think at all about number facts.
Man has learned to prepare for future needs.
Of food, clothing and fuel accumulation is agreed.
Just about all rodents collect and store food.
They don't think, it being instinct rather than mood.
The development of speech was how abstract thinking began.
Words represented things or actions to early man.
To form complex words man combined simple sounds.
Then modifiers meant accurate descriptions would abound.
Man developed the idea of counting along the way.
Number equivalence became apparent one day.
Three fingers could represent three dogs or deer.
When relaying information, the message would be clear.
With words you can picture things in your mind,

Then relay the information to the rest of mankind.
You can create stories or picture the reason why,
And one day explain the wonder of the sky.

2. Fine Motor Skills

We didn't need fine motor skills throughout our past.
Early man's tools were rocks and sticks they grasped.
Something changed between then and the modern day.
We gained the ability to manipulate small thing along the way,
Needles and thread, tweezers, pencils and pens.
Surgeons operate on ears and replace the eye lens.
Watch makers repair the tiniest working parts.
Many are skilled at various crafts and arts.
We may lose this ability in the coming age.
Kids' writing doesn't improve from the elementary stage.
But who needs to write when you can text?
Only thumbs get the workout. What's next?
Thinking back, man did have a fine motor need,
When picking small berries and various type seeds.
Also, they helped out their fellows-quite nice.
They groomed, meaning picking out fleas and lice.
Maybe this was the start. It would suffice.

3. Man Adapts

Many animals adapt when conditions change.
I'm thinking of when man encroaches on their range.
Some even do better living close to man.
The new conditions interfere with predators' plans.
The most adaptable are rats, you'd probably guess.
Though pigeons do as well making cities a mess.

For radical changes resulting in a species advance,
They have to wait for the evolutionary chance.
Some mutation may allow them to survive more cold or heat,
To prosper out of water or later retreat.
Of all species now inhabiting our earth,
Man is the most adaptable, not by birth.
Any changes in man happened eons ago.
Call it chance, nature or God made it so.
For 50,000 years it's thought we've been the same.
That's the time of the great exodus, from Africa we came.
Apparently, in Africa we lived on the veldt.
Relatively hot and dry, the eastern grassland belt.
Through his intelligence man has adapted quite well,
Where it's cold beyond belief or hot as hell.
Man can move in the water or fly in the sky,
And eat almost anything that happens to come by.
We're the most adaptable by far you could say,
And yet we didn't mutate to get this way.
We're the same essentially as the beginning day.

4. Defining Man

Anthropologists used to waste effort defining man.
Figure what's different between species if you can.
First they thought of man, the user of tools.
Several animals do, so they felt like fools.
Then man, the maker of tools held sway.
After observing chimps, to this it was nay.
Maybe it's man the builder of structures, but no.
Beavers and muskrats plus bee types have those.
Is it language? Dolphins and whales seem to converse.
Even dogs get meaning across, body language not verse.

Is it man who alone seems to have future plans?
Many rodents save food for when winter hits the land.
Surely man is notable for environmental change.
The wonder of beaver dam building isn't so strange.
I have one definition we share with no other.
Man wears clothing, not true of any animal brother.
We have no hair to insulate and protect our skin.
Clothes are almost as good as hair of our animal kin.

5. The Separation

Several million years ago, chimps separated from man.
Picture our ancestors as knuckle walkers if you can.
For some reason they left the forest to live on the plains.
There was more predator danger. What did they gain?
Here were our ancestors, slow and relatively light
With no claws or horns with which to fight.
The rain forest provided a variety of food.
Life for our ancestors should have been good.
They could only survive in groups to conquer fears.
To drive away hyenas and lions, they needed spears.
Maybe control of fire helped them survive.
Could throwing rocks mean they would stay alive?
I have a strong feeling early man was pretty smart.
He invented tools and controlled fire from the start.
Otherwise, leaving the forest would spell his end,
And human history would have stopped right then.

6. First Immigrants

We have this penchant of naming ourselves and our kin
After one of our forebears country of origin.
Italian-American, Polish, African or German.

Except Native Americans. It's easier to say Indians.
They were misnamed by early explorers, not a slur.
Those being wildly confused about where they were.
If hyphenated Americans are how we are all named,
Then Indians should be Siberian-Americans from whence they came.
There is a theory on how they emigrated here.
Sea levels were low due to glaciation in a long past year.
So much water was contained in ice on land
That the Bering Strait was crossed by an adventurous band.
It's assumed that there must have been an ice free path.
So that they could walk south avoiding winter's wrath.
I can picture crossing a temporary land bridge.
Not an ice free corridor amidst nature's fridge.
I'm sure the adventurers brought their stuff.
Modern travelers know you can never bring enough.
They had to carry their tools and fire making kit.
Blankets, hunting implements, food to last a bit.
Plus, babies and toddlers, some water just in case.
Scouts ran ahead seeking the next resting place.
No beasts of burden, no wheeled carts to ease the way.
They surely needed good hunting almost every day.
At that time in history with the Ice Age cold,
They just couldn't make it no matter how bold.
An alternative theory is to forget the long hike.
They could have come by boat. This theory I like.
Think of the advantages, further travel each day.
Seals and other game were available along the way.
Plus, they could take all their stuff with room to spare.
Seal skin would provide for shelter and clothes to wear.
Some would claim they couldn't know how to build a boat.

Don't forget dugouts, kayaks, canoes all nicely float.
Siberian-Americans developed these we can note.

7. Eskimos of Old

In this wide world who's the toughest of men?
To me those who fit are Eskimos and their kin.
Those who live on Greenland's northern coast
Have the toughest life. Of trials they have the most.
Winter could cause depression with a half year dark.
No sun to cheer them. Nothing to give life a spark.
No real source of heat, a seal oil lamp for light.
Equivalent to a candle to keep back the night.
They never eat dairy, vegetables or any fruit.
In fact they never see anything green, no leaf or shoot.
They eat only fish and animals that eat the same.
All of this raw, with no way to cook the game.
Their igloos are tiny. They must be kept cold as ice.
With no building material, compact snow must suffice.
Seal skin provides their blankets and clothes.
These protect them from mother natures extreme blows.
They have no metal, Tools are made from bone.
Tribal groups are small. They are so alone.
They build their kayaks with drift wood and skin,
And hunt seals and whales, death if they fall in.
The kayaks have a cover in case of overturn.
To right the kayak, the Eskimo must quickly learn.
The north is unforgiving, Their life is a wonder.
Eskimos are cheerful knowing they must never blunder.

8. Two Great Inventions

Some claim the greatest early inventions were fire and
the wheel.
Fire was important, but I must relate how I feel.
The wheel is way down the list after building of roads.
Which weren't necessary 'til men moved big loads.
Fire allowed people to eat a bigger variety of food.
Skewer it, bake it on coals, it was easier chewed.
Fire lit the night and kept predators at bay.
Keeping you warm in winter, I conclude, no way.
Winter campers know fire may keep your front hot,
For the back side, the benefit is definitely not.
So fire didn't allow man to move from the tropics.
Fire is overrated. Now on to other topics.
The invention of clothing and shelter top my list.
On cold, wet nights they helped early man exist.
For shelter, caves helped. They're not everywhere.
Thus, man used leaves, thatch or bark tied with care.
Their buildings weren't wind proof, but kept them dry.
Animal skin tents were an improvement by and by.
The most important invention by any measure at all
Was clothing. Maybe the result of man's fall.
Man's portable shelter kept him dry and warm.
It protected him from sun, insects, scratches and other
harm.
Clothing allowed man to live in climate extreme
From deserts to the Arctic and be supreme.
The only thing available was animal skin,
So tanning and sewing were the invention's kin.
Clothing is one thing that separates animals from man.
With it we are masters of the land.

9. Containers

Animals don't have the ability to carry much stuff.
What room in their mouths is not space enough.
If it's one object, they can drag it away,
Like the leopard saving its kill for another day.
A monkey or an ape will fill its mouth and hands,
Then walk awkwardly as its balance demands.
No animal can carry water away from its source.
If one of its tribe can't walk, it'll die in due course.
One of our great ancestors got the bright idea.
He invented the container. From thirst he was free.
Animal bladders were probably used this way.
They were natural containers in which liquids would stay.
After that came animal skin, bark and woven reeds.
Wooden slats, vines and clay to fill their needs.
The gatherers could carry food back to their huts,
Roots, fruit and berries, acorns and nuts.
They could save food for the cold winter day.
Containers allowed them to prosper this way.
Among the great inventions containers hold sway.

10. Domestication

It's relatively easy to catch animals that are small.
Though before iron it wasn't easy to cage them all.
A wood fence won't stop a mammal that can dig or chew.
However, bird's feathers can be trimmed through.
Once birds are captured and trimmed they'll stay,
As long as they're enclosed and can't get away.
How about larger animals like the wild horse?
Dogs most likely helped herd them in due course.
What brilliant mind thought a horse would carry a pack,

Pull a load, or allow a man to ride on its back?
Yet horses were tamed. We allayed their fears,
And they helped man for thousands of years.
We domesticated more to work or fight in our battles,
Donkeys, camels, buffalo, llamas, reindeer, cattle.
Finally, there's the elephant. How was the first caught?
I can't figure how. My ideas come to naught.
Now they use trained elephants to catch those wild,
Only the females and those without child.
For more than two millennia they've been used in war,
Scaring enemy soldiers to their very core.
The Carthaginians used them in attacking Rome,
And Alexander faced them in India far from home.
The ancients had the skill to catch and tame.
I expect the modern day techniques are the same.

11. Domesticated Dogs

Dozens of animals have been domesticated by man.
Dogs were the first, though I'm sure it wasn't planned.
I think that wolves may have come close to see
What humans were doing. They didn't flee.
One man threw a bone to chase them away.
Wolves descendants have been begging to this day.
The thrown bone was handed over up close.
One man and one wolf were braver than most.
The relationship blossomed for the benefit of all.
The wolves became our friends for the long haul.
It's mysterious and a wonder. It's like we're a pack.
Dogs over the millennia have worked with brains and back.
Man with selective breeding, a sign of intelligence
Has developed dogs to work in every sense,

From rat terriers, herders, war dogs and hunters too,
They worked with man as we wanted them to do.
Most are now pets. Why are they there?
To love us and protect us in return for our care.
We dog owners know, it's a bargain that's fair.

12. Domesticating Plants

It's an activity many do at least once a week.
We visit the supermarket for the food we seek.
All should be awed by the choices there.
In the distant past these shelves would be bare.
We have fruits and vegetables from dozens of climes.
Where did they all come from in ancient times?
Every plant represented grew wild back then.
Primitive people gathered food as it had always been.
Brilliant ones among them realized the purpose of seed.
And tried planting them to provide for future need.
They found that caring for plants increased yields.
Soon they were farmers with crops in their fields.
The smart ones looked for properties that would suit.
More output per acre, better taste, bigger fruit.
For example all the corn, tomatoes, potatoes and peppers were derived
In the Americas well before Europeans arrived.
Over the ages we have the results of careful selection.
The many food varieties making a great collection.
Primitives started it. We still strive for perfection.

13. Sheep to the Rescue

No one much wonders about domestication of sheep.
Why was so much effort expended, these to keep?
I think ancient men thought of sheepskin's roll
In providing thick fleece to keep out the cold.
Now comes the interesting part of our tale.
True genius showed on a monumental scale.
First came the discovery, twisting wool together made yarn.
What use could this have? They would later learn.
The great idea was the weaving invention.
Were they thinking of clothing? Was it their intention?
Now if you cut a wool blanket just so,
A garment resulted when pieces were sown.
The advantages were twofold when this was tried.
No hunting required and no animals killed for their hide.
Later other fibers were discovered to fill the need,
Flax, silk, and cotton, finally men did succeed
With manufacturing fibers, the most desirable it's agreed.

14. Ancient Stone Works

No one knows for sure why the pyramids were made.
The pharaohs wanted monuments that wouldn't fade.
The great stone piles would last for eternity.
Markers that the Gods would surely see.
What they constructed was truly a wonder,
Though the desert wind will ultimately plunder.
People have questioned how all the stones were moved.
Get enough rollers, slaves, and rope. This can't be disproved.
The construction is a wonder but more importantly,

How were the stones prepared, three sides to cut free?
Bronze was the hardest metal that they had.
Their tools couldn't last, the sharp edge going bad.
And yet the Egyptians cut millions of stones,
We can count the cost in slave workers bones.
Structures are equally impressive in the west.
The Mayans, Aztecs and Incas were the best.
They used no rollers and had no tough metal tools.
Yet they built their pyramids being far from fools.
High in the Andes, Incas built of stone.
These were unbelievable, their skill shone.
The stones aren't rectangular, the easy way,
But they fit together perfectly as they lay.
Less than a knife blade separates them to this day.

Chapter 9. Human Wonders

Ah! The human condition, tough but we get by.
We manage. Sometimes I wonder how and why.

1. Group Invention

All through history progress was made with the idea.
People working alone didn't leave things be.
Maybe way back no one started out to invent.
Was each new development heaven sent?
An accidental happening, the luck of the draw,
And a single person was aware and saw.
For an example, an extra hot fire built on sand,
Viola, glass. Millennia later results were grand.
For the first observer maybe a sharp edge was found,
Then came windows, jars and lenses were ground.
Perhaps more than one were in collusion.
Try this or that, 'til there was a suitable conclusion.
Edison, the greatest inventor, showed the way.
Get a bunch of people to think and try for pay.
Then came the research labs of recent years
Where developing ideas became their careers.
Unimaginable developments were hatched this way.
Can we improve on this in future days?
What if we had millions included world wide,
Thinking about an idea on a scientific side?
Would you think, no way, no how?
With the internet it's happening right now.

2. Thrill of Discovery

As good parents, we want to protect our kids from harm,
And give them guidance for a life that's charmed.
Don't swim alone, be careful on the street,
Use your head with strangers who you meet.
Don't smoke, don't drink, don't use drugs,
Take care of your stuff, steer clear of thugs.
It's certainly desirable to protect your young.
It would be great if their praises were sung.
I feel it's the duty of every mom and dad
To prepare them for real life, good or bad.
Kids should learn it's all right to fail.
Life can be mild or stormy with gales.
However, they shouldn't be taught 'til completely filled.
They need to experience discovery's thrill.
Discover the wonder of all that's around.
To spot what's out there ready to be found.
Maybe the greatest gift you can bestow
Is to keep a child's wonder all aglow.
As they age there's still much to know.

3. The Brain

The human brain, the most wondrous thing we know.
This will remain true no matter how far we go.
I become more aware of this fact as I age.
Though scientists study it, they're at the beginning stage.
The basic question, how is information stored?
How is it retrieved from this massive data hoard?
How does the brain put data together in a thought,
Combining sights, sounds, names, other information sought?

Why do you forget a name or maybe a word?
A background search goes on not being spurred.
At a later time you remember the missing fact.
How does the brain do this wonderful act?
I have a mental exercise when seeking sleep,
Remembering people's names from the past most deep.
An unknown one will come to me in a bit.
It will arrive even though I'm not seeking it.
The brain stores data in unbelievable amounts.
Faces, scenes, words, voices, more than you can count.
Meanwhile it keeps the body on automatic pilot.
You can do so many things without conscious thought.
You can walk, talk, and chew gum at the same time.
Brushing teeth, shaving, combing hair while not in your prime.
If you had to think every time you drove a car,
You wouldn't be able to go very far.
Unconsciously, every decision made is controlled by the brain.
If you had to think of all the details, you'd go insane.
They know from various scans the brains active parts.
When doing a given task, this is but the start.
They know adult brains are different from teens.
Big deal. We know this from other means.
The brain will remain an enigma, so it seems.

4. Our Wonderful Senses

Our senses are a wonder don't you agree.
Pity the man who looks and does not see.
Is he aware of a smile or the glory of a flowering tree?
Pity the man who listens but does not hear.
For him no bird song or baby laugh will cheer.

Pity the man who's touched but does not feel.
Will he know how a lover's caress can heal?
Pity the man who eats but does not taste.
For him the chef's careful preparation is a waste.
Pity the man who breathes but does not smell.
Will he know the stories the aromas tell?
Our senses are the window to all out there.
It's how the world's wonders are shared.

5. Moving Toward Danger

The fastest runners had crossed the finish line.
Fortunately, spectators had thinned by this time.
When the bombs went off, the cameras caught the scene.
The blasts were directed where many had been.
I watched the reaction. People ducked and started to run.
Then they turned to see, almost every one.
Each stopped and returned to help those in need.
Of the natural survival reaction, they took no heed.
They helped the wounded and stopped the blood.
Sometimes just holding a hand, they did what they could.
What makes a human ignore danger to do good?
They helped strangers, the ultimate good deed.
This wonderful "Boston Strong" should be everyone's creed.
Remember this but also remember the evil ones,
Who kill the infidel, innocents both adult and young.

6. Finders Keepers?

"My damn gut is starting to moan and groan.
I haven't eaten today. I should have known.
I had food last night. I shared it with Flynn.

He needed it more than me. He's just bones and skin.
I'll try that dumpster behind the bar and grill.
Maybe I shouldn't be here. In the afternoon I can get my
fill.
Hell it's empty. The garbage truck came early today.
Some places I find food, but they chase me away.
I once was given a meal prepared just for me,
Not made up from plate scrapings, and it was free.
Well, no good deed goes unpunished seems to be the rule.
That good man was fired. Helping made him a fool.
I'll amble over to the park, check out the cans.
Young people eat there, then change their plans.
Sometimes they'll chuck a sandwich or some fruit.
Well, in all these cans there's nothing that suits.
What's this? Someone left this nice new pack.
I'll check inside. Maybe I can bring it back.
Oh, Lordie. There's cash here and travelers checks.
Easy street! But then my life would be a wreck.
Keeping this would be stealing which I've never done.
I'll have to do what's right. That's rule number one.
I'll take it to the cops. They'll know what to do.
It's too big a burden. I'm glad to be through."
What makes a penniless man do this noble thing,
When you think what benefits it would bring?
With all the dishonesty we see every day,
It's a wonder when the story works the other way.

7. Maybe It's Love

Why does a guy work his tail off at a dirty job,
While he sees some neighbor who's a lazy slob.
Should he also fake an injury and live on the dole?
Not this guy. Such behavior would rot his soul.

What makes a guy risk his life helping another?
He doesn't even know him. It's not his brother.
Why does someone dive into a lake to save a child?
He can't swim well. He doesn't ever act wild.
Why does one stop to help at the side of the road?
While most keep going no desire to be slowed?
Why run into a burning building, maybe you'll die.
Because someone may be there. Did you hear a cry?
Evolutionary theory can't explain the how and the why.
We're supposed to seek survival. We don't want to die.
Most animals protect their young, keep them from harm.
For the rest of their kind it's enough to sound the alarm.
With people some are heroic, maybe it's a lot.
They'll instinctively do what's right like as not.
And maybe it's love to give all you've got.

8. Luck of the Draw

With all the sickness available it's wonder any are alive.
Maybe to be completely healthy's too much for which to strive.
There are dozens of pathogens ready to strike,
Plus dozens more, autoimmune ones and the like.
Most of the old pathogens are controlled.
It's the new ones that are taking hold,
Like Lyme disease and SARS to name two.
And those that resist antibiotics, MRSA is new.
Old folks may have some immunity. For what it's worth
We lived close to animals and played in the dirt.
Still, with all this we mostly die from the big three,
Heart attacks, cancers and strokes are these.
Luckily, we do have some control if we try.
We can improve our chances postponing when we die.

Basically, live a healthy life. Follow the rules.
Avoid the harmful substances though they seem cool.
For most cancers and the autoimmune stuff,
The healthy practices are just not enough.
For these you need luck in good measure.
This wonderful gift you can fully treasure.

9. Cheerful in Death

He was new to the ward, the comatose old guy.
Everyone there knew he would soon die.
The medical staff wouldn't spend much time with him.
If he woke, he'd be a gomer. His outlook dim.
All were surprised when they heard his calling bell.
He welcomed the young nurse and wished her well.
He complimented her beauty, what a surprise.
Another, the morning sun sparkled in her eyes.
The orderly who cleaned his room each day
Talked with him. He usually hadn't much to say.
The brusk doctor talked about personal things
And got some advise, "Time flies on wings.
Take the time to spend with each kid.
They grow so fast, you'll be glad you did."
He always smiled and said hello to people passing by.
Patients, visitors, and staff waved to the guy.
The wonder was happiness spread to the whole ward,
Or maybe it was just more human, thank the Lord.
When he died more than one shed tears.
His brief time brought in a bit of cheer.

10. Laughing at Misfortune

Sometimes you can raise spirits by sharing a laugh.
Maybe some of that depression can be lowered by half.
I've often wondered why more old folks don't feel low.
Certainly in late life you receive enough blows.
You can always get a chuckle with "hearing" jokes.
"What's that, your hearing aid's starting to smoke?"
How do you tell an old duffer his zipper is down?
Saying it loud enough will bring a few frowns.
Though the humor of the situation can bring a laugh,
The person isn't named who made the gaff.
We can laugh at the misfortune, "I've got a trick knee,
Which means I can't do stand up comedy."
"Watch out. Fall and you can wind up dead."
"Nothing to worry about if I land on my head."
One old crank was not liked so well.
"John has Alzheimers." "Oh, how can you tell?"
We love to gather and each wants a say.
Interrupting each other freely, none asks if they may.
However, if one is slow and can't get the words out,
All become quiet. We listen. He has no need to shout.
Sometimes the conversation takes a morbid turn.
The ideas expressed, young people would probably spurn.
Though normally not funny, we can laugh.
We're laughing at death, we're not daft.

11. Sixteen Years

I just passed my 80th year of age.
What a wonder that I've turned another page.
Now 80 is divisible by 16 and 5.
Consider these are segments I've been alive.

Sixteen years since my retirement, oh dear,
These have zipped past, a decade is like a year.
I think of that first segment back in the day.
Then, time moved so slowly along the way.
Physical changes were the biggest during this time.
New born to full height, then I was in my prime.
I could jump higher, climb faster up a rope.
Do more pull ups, run up a steep slope.
Then I learned the most important lesson of all.
To always pick myself up when I'd fall.
Toddlers do this naturally. There's no thought.
It just gets harder, the lesson must be re-taught.
The next segment was when the big milestones were made.
Most important, marrying my wife. Our love won't fade.
During this time, we bore our kids four.
Parenthood was for us. Our babies we adored.
Lesser milestones, high school graduation and as time flew,
Later a BS, an MS and a PhD too.
In that segment I satisfied my military career.
We bought our house, we've lived here 49 years.
In the third segment, three of our kids finished high school,
Starting the big expense time, depleting the money pool.
I changed jobs, a major milestone for me,
Becoming a rocket scientist, what I'd hoped to be.
The fourth segment also was an eventful one.
All four kids married, their schooling all done.
All in their houses, grand kids born, nine of ten.
Finally, the old man was done. Leave the job to younger men.
The last segment has no milestones for me.
The kids and grand kids have enough you see.

I'll postpone that final milestone as long as can be.

12. I'm the One Who Helps

I'm used to being the one who helps out.
The kids could count on me with no doubt.
When they were younger with no money, I fixed their cars.
I crossed my fingers hoping they would go far.
We helped them move in and out of school.
Later it was a family operation, pretty cool.
Changing apartments, moving to a new abode.
We got together, many Hands would carry the load.
I got a new task, the last time they moved.
Assembling the crib and beds, my skill was proved.
My daughter-in-law didn't say, but thought of my age.
I accepted her suggestion, the advise of a young sage.
However, I continued to work on kids' houses and my own.
The biggest project doubled the size of one son's home.
At 70 I shingled most of our house's roof.
I've retired from construction. To this I'm now aloof.
Always I've helped the kids when there was a need.
Being the safe harbor is our enduring creed,
Though at 80, I know I must limit the good deeds.

13. They Need Me

Is it possible to will yourself well,
Knowing that with aging it all goes to hell?
I swear that having to take care of my wife
Does something to lengthen my life.
It doesn't burden me. I take her wherever she goes.

She no longer drives. My willingness she knows.
I've taken over the laundry, cleaning and dishes.
I fetch things up or down whatever her wishes.
I take her shopping mostly for the food.
She knows the rest puts me in a bad mood.
We also have a little dog who needs care.
Whenever she goes out, I'm the one there,
Two short trips and two long walks per day.
This exercise keeps me healthy you could say.
I keep active physically and mentally too.
Luck has helped, or alternately I have a clue.
Why have I avoided those diseases that hit the old?
I'm healthy 'cause they need me, truth be told.

14. The I Don't Care Stage

I know I have a limited number of hours.
I'd rather use them smelling the flowers,
Instead of keeping up with all the modern stuff.
That's what I don't care about. My interests are enough.
A great plethora of gadgets are out there.
About the latest tablet or cell, I don't care.
Some of these things are rotting peoples' minds.
With too much use, they are addictive you'll find.
I've read there's no need for memorization now.
You can find anything on the internet somehow.
We are the sum of our memories in the main.
Maybe there are too many factoids in our brains.
I'd rather sit and talk, no worry about what's next.
I don't play with some app, e-mail or text.
Some young folks would consider me out of touch.
Yet I know more about literature, history, geography and such.

I won't even go into science about which I'm aware.
I know of the wondrous developments out there.
When I have a need, I Google information on the net.
I use my cell for emergencies, it's a good bet.
I have no desire to constantly keep in touch.
I'm interested in people's news, but not that much.
Personal conversations, snail mail, or the land line
Are good enough for me. I find each just fine.

15. The Wonderful Life

The greatest gift you can have in your life,
Be blessed with true love between husband and wife.
By true love I mean that which can adapt and grow.
We certainly aren't static as the decades go.
Neither partner can expect the other to remain the same.
We definitely don't stay 25 in life's game.
You do things for each other asked or not.
You share your pleasure and hurts whatever your lot.
You spend time together. When you must be apart,
You want the separation over. It pains your heart.
At the end of the work day, you can't wait to get home.
You have absolutely no desire to roam.
Your interests don't need to be all the same.
She likes to sew, he watches a football game.
When you feel anger, learn to hold your tongue.
What has upset you, your spouse isn't the one.
If something bothers you, gently speak your mind.
With every reprimand remember always be kind.
Don't let little things bother your day.
Being a grievance collector is never the way.
With a good attitude and if luck smiles on you,
You'll spend a gifted life together as two.

And if you share love with your offspring,
This is the connection that between past and future brings.
If all goes well, they'll also find true love,
And pass this on to their kids with help from above.

16. Am I Selfish?

We are old. There's no getting around this.
Old age doesn't come alone, though there's still bliss.
We both expect we'll live less than ten years.
We still give and get love, friendship and cheer.
With many old couples the first one dies,
And the second soon follows, no surprise.
They are completely devoted, lovers, best friends.
There's no reason to live, the second life ends.
With us, we both want the other to live,
Make a new life, both having much to give.
We know that our lover will be gone,
But that new love can grow with the dawn.
I know if I outlive my lovely wife,
I'll have more time to remember a great life.
I can thank her for a life full of joy.
She'll know that death this won't destroy.
Am I selfish to want to have more time?
I still have myself to give. It's no crime.

17. My Dearest Love

My dearest love, how time has flown.
I am the luckiest of all women I've known.
Our love has blossomed for all these years.
So much happiness, companionship, so few tears.

How lucky am I, and I thank God above
For giving me you to treasure and love.
Through all the years, we never had lots of money.
But, as the song goes, "It didn't matter, honey."
With our beloved children our lives have been blessed.
Then came our precious grand babies, a joy not to be missed.
As the years wind down, I want you to know
I've treasured every minute of our 58 year "show."
Oh, how I adore being your wife.
I'll love you beyond forever my soul mate, friend for life.
I Love You,
Suz
PS.
So much appreciation, sweetheart for a happy life,
And taking such good care of your dizzy wife.